# TEN THOUGHTS TO TAKE INTO ETERNITY

## *Living Wisely in Light of the Afterlife*

# DR. DAVID YOUNT

SIMON & SCHUSTER

SIMON & SCHUSTER
Rockefeller Center
1230 Avenue of the Americas
New York, NY 10020

SIMON & SCHUSTER and colophon are
registered trademarks of Simon & Schuster Inc.

*Designed by Ruth Lee*

Manufactured in the United States of America

1   3   5   7   9   10   8   6   4   2

Library of Congress Cataloging-in-Publication Data

Yount, D.D., David.
Ten thoughts to take into eternity : living wisely
in light of the afterlife / David Yount, D.D.
p.    cm.
Includes bibliographical references.
1. Future life. 2. Near-death experiences. I. Title.
BL535.Y68      1999
291.2'3—dc21        98-54833  CIP

ISBN 0-684-82420-5

To the memory of

*Ernest Wittenberg*

Blessed be He who has mercy upon his creatures.
Blessed be He who pays a good reward to those who fear Him.

Into paradise may the angels lead you
and bring you into the holy city Jerusalem.

# CONTENTS

One short sleep past, we wake eternally,
And death shall be no more. Death, thou shalt die.

JOHN DONNE

The key to immortality is to lead a life worth living.

SAINT AUGUSTINE

# TEN THOUGHTS
# TO TAKE INTO
# ETERNITY

# A BETTER PLACE

B EFORE HE BECAME BRITAIN'S LORD CHANCELLOR, THE LATE
F. E. Smith was a brash young barrister much taken with his
own disputation. One day in court he was interrupted by an exasperated judge, who pleaded, "Mr. Smith, you have been talking
now for ten minutes, and I am none the wiser."

"None the wiser perhaps, my lord," Smith politely replied,
"but better informed."

With this book I have an even grander ambition than the lord
chancellor's—not only to better inform you about our mutual
prospects for life after death, but to enable us both to be wiser
about living our present lives in the light of eternity.

When pressed, most authors will confess that they write for
themselves, sharing with their readers what they have learned
about a subject that fascinates them. I am no exception. Although
I have written for publication all my adult life, I postponed attempting a book until I turned sixty, when, prompted by a sense
of my own mortality, I began to reexamine beliefs I had held since
childhood, to determine whether they still stood up to scrutiny
and could support the weight of my remaining years.

Initially I tackled the foundations of faith itself (in the book
*Growing in Faith*), then the efficacy of prayer (in *Breaking Through
God's Silence*), and finally the practicality of spiritual living (in

*Spiritual Simplicity*). But I was left with the realization that every human being must confront mortality itself and its consequences—eternal life or oblivion—and the sooner the better, so as to live the remainder of his or her days meaningfully.

When, in middle age, I consulted my doctor about a variety of minor complaints, he noted that the human body ages like an automobile. First it loses its luster and begins to display scratches and dents; then the mechanism itself develops squeaks and rattles. Eventually a vital part fails that either can't be replaced or isn't worth fixing, and it's off to the auto graveyard.

With this analogy, my doctor was only counseling proper health maintenance on my part, but his lecture brought me face-to-face with my own mortality and the question whether there is life beyond death. For a writer, the best way to confront inevitability is to write about it.

For such a fascinating subject—one that applies to literally every man, woman, and child—life after death has attracted surprisingly scant treatment in scholarship. On the one side there is serious theology about the resurrection; but it is persuasive only to Christians. On the other there lies a vast literature of the obscure and the occult—murky to navigate, much of it wishful thinking, some of it quackery.

I first approached the subject of eternity in *Breaking Through God's Silence,* thanks to my wife, who drew my attention to responsible studies of near-death and out-of-body experiences. Inasmuch as people ultimately pray for eternal life, it seemed to make sense to explore the object of their yearning. Near-death accounts, joined by a rereading of Dante, Milton, Chesterton, Shaw, William James, C. S. Lewis, and others, led me to attempt this book. Swiss theologian Hans Küng's nine public lectures on eternity, delivered at the University of Michigan in 1983, further stimulated my thinking and suggested many other sources.

In addition, for the first time in my life, I seriously approached the genre of science fiction for clues it might offer about a new heaven and a new earth. If the "new creation" is (as even many Christians suspect) but an alteration of humankind's current situation, then there are many authors outside the cloister who are already applying their imaginations to the question "What if?" and yielding provocative answers. Revealingly, the *Star Trek* series and their spin-offs appeal disproportionately to educated adults, not to children.

At the end of our lives, you and I will be joining the vast majority of peoples who have passed from this life before us. My parents have long since been laid to rest along with every close relative save one. So many friends and colleagues have already passed from this life, some of them while still young, the victims of disease and accident, a few of suicide. As the years pass, my list of remembrance grows longer.

The poet Robert Browning insisted against death that "the best is yet to be." If that is your expectation (as it is mine), then the present life is simply a prelude and should be lived in the prospect of eternity. In the chapters that follow I offer ten thoughts you may wish to take with you, but only after applying them to give meaning to your life now.

$$\mathcal{B}\mathcal{D}$$

As he lay dying, Tony promised his beloved Maria an eternity of love with her, free from the cares of mortal time. The young hero of *West Side Story* was but an updated version of Shakespeare's Romeo, who, believing his Juliet to be dead, rushed to join her in eternity, exclaiming:

> O, here
> *Will I set up my everlasting rest,*
> *And shake the yoke of inauspicious stars*
> *From this world-wearied flesh.*

In *A Tale of Two Cities,* Sidney Carton approached his execution certain that "it is a far, far better rest that I go to, than I have ever known." Charles Dickens wrote of the condemned hero that his "was the peacefullest man's face ever beheld."

In real life, distinct from books and plays, few of us break into song or verse as we breathe our last, but the expectation of resuming life in a better place is timeless and universal. Even skeptics agree with the late pianist Glenn Gould that eternal life is infinitely preferable to its alternative—oblivion. Asked, "Where do we go from here?" most Americans agree with the hopeful refrain of *West Side Story* that it will be "Somewhere."

For millions of credible persons now living, the afterlife is not just a hopeful hypothesis but an actual experience. Somehow revived after having been medically dead, these men, women, and children report not only that death is kind but that eternal bliss awaits. They know, they insist, because they have been there. Having resumed their earthly lives among us, they are transformed, living not for the present but in the light and expectation of eternity.

Astronomer Carl Sagan was an expert on living. In fact, he is the author of the article "Life" in the *Encyclopaedia Britannica.* Yet several years before Sagan's death, in 1996, he suffered a near-death experience—and surprisingly enough spoke well of it: "I would recommend almost dying to everybody. You get a much clearer perspective on what's important and what isn't."

Accounts like his have brought the singular event of near-death experiences to the forefront of our collective consciousness. However, in the years before the experience became well known, many persons were hesitant to reveal them. Although her 1973 near-death experience would become celebrated in her best-seller, *Embraced by the Light,* Betty Eadie waited nineteen years to report the event. Jean Smith, who nearly died in 1952, had never heard of such an experience and so initially kept it a secret from everyone but her parents—who dismissed her report as delusional.

Interestingly, though, both women had positive things to say about the frontier of eternity. Smith's husband believed her account but was understandably hurt when his wife confessed that, having tasted eternity, she didn't want to return to earthly life.

Melvin Moore, M.D., author of the acclaimed *Transformed by the Light,* further validates Smith's and Eadie's experiences. According to his research, millions of people around the world have had near-death experiences—and incredibly, all who return from death's door embrace everyday living and lose their fear of death. Some even appear to develop psychic powers and enhanced intelligence.

In addition, those who return consistently live significantly healthier lives, use fewer medications, miss less time from work, and are more securely employed than the average person. Moreover, they are largely immune from depression and anxiety. Although people who have undergone near-death experiences are more attracted to solitude and meditation than even the average churchgoer, they also volunteer more in their communities and give more of their income to charity than the average American.

Dr. Morse reports that near-death experiences are generally characterized by nine traits (although few people report all nine). These experiences include

1. *A sense of being dead,* which many describe as the experience of being unfettered and totally themselves.
2. *Peace and painlessness,* a consciousness of earthly surroundings while feeling detached from them.
3. *Out-of-body experience,* being a spectator rather than an actor, hovering over one's own body.
4. *Tunnel experience,* a feeling of being sucked into a tunnel that has an exit.

5. *People of light.* One emerges from the tunnel into brilliance, where people glow from an inner light.
6. *Being of light.* One meets a being who glows, nourishes, and loves.
7. *Life review,* in which one personally experiences the joy and hurt he or she caused others in life.
8. *Reluctance to return* to one's earthly body.
9. *Personality transformation,* with a new perspective and appreciation, and a sense of being connected to the entire universe.

Have these people seen God? Few who have ventured to the edge, whether simple or sophisticated, even attempt to analyze their experience, because they find it incomparable. When asked about the light she saw, one woman told Dr. Morse, "It wasn't God, but it wasn't *not* God."

By contrast, Angie Fenimore was sure of God's presence when she went to the edge, but it was a fearful experience, because she was a suicide. In *Beyond the Darkness* this wife and mother recounts how she slashed her wrists and poisoned herself in a quest for oblivion. As she was dying, she felt suspended in darkness, wrapped in a waist-high black mist that held her prisoner:

> It had life, this darkness, some kind of intelligence that was purely negative, even evil. It sucked at me, pulling me to react, and then swallowing my reaction into fear and dread. In my life I had suffered pain and despair so great that I could barely function, but the twisting anguish of this disconnection was beyond my capacity to conceive.

She sensed that she was in hell, a place where hope came to die. "Is this what you really want?" God's voice thundered. The suffering was different from the agonies of life, she relates. It was "pointless, redundant, and stifling." This, she surmised, was the "never-ending torment that awaited me for taking my own life." When she revived, she concluded that hell, while a real experience, is "primarily a state of mind. . . . I had been in hell long before I died, and I hadn't realized it, because I had escaped many of the consequences up until the point that I took my life."

When Angie returned to this world of physical pain, she was relieved and overwhelmed with gratitude: "I felt like Ebenezer Scrooge, having been granted a warning glimpse of my fate; and then, once I understood, having been given a second chance."

"Learn to die and thou shalt learn to live," counsels the medieval *Ars moriendi,* or *Art of Dying.* It is a lesson well learned by those who have tasted death. They gain an appetite for living, give generously of themselves, and approach their definitive demise with an equanimity, hope, and confidence that the rest of us can only dream of acquiring. Because they have been to the edge already and found the journey exhilarating, they do not fear the return trip.

How credible is the near-death experience? Is it really an experience of eternity? Long before the publication of popular accounts of such experiences, they were being studied by the scientific community. More than twenty years of research has documented that they are natural occurrences and not hallucinations. Scientists have even identified the area of the brain in which the experience occurs.

While none of the research can definitively settle the question of whether or not those who undergo near-death experiences actually encounter eternity, it does suggest that death need not be feared and that eternity offers the fullness of life that religious faith has always promised.

While recent authors who have made their near-death accounts public are often inarticulate in attempting to explain their extraordinary visions, others before them described their *real-death* experiences poignantly. With his last words, Thomas Edison reported that "it is very beautiful over there." "I've never felt better," confided Douglas Fairbanks. "I feel myself again," said Sir Walter Scott. Elizabeth Barrett Browning's final word as she met death was, "Beautiful!" Goethe exclaimed, "More light!" Chopin observed, "Now I am at the source of all blessedness." Rousseau, ever verbose, urged those who attended him to "see the sun, whose smiling face calls me; see that immeasurable light. There is God! Yes, God himself, who is opening his arms and inviting me to taste at last that eternal and unchanging joy that I have so long desired." These celebrated men and women, who had much to live for, nevertheless took leave of this life with the conviction that they were entering a better one.

Short of being transported to eternity in a near-death experience, there are other ways you and I can anticipate it—through immersion in the present moment, and through our sense of loss. People of faith agree that the closest experience to eternity is living totally immersed in the present moment. Eternity, after all, is an inexhaustible *now,* embracing past and future.

This is not as mystical as it seems. The awkwardness with life this side of eternity is that we preoccupy ourselves with regret for the past and anxiety about the future. For most of us, the present moment is only a fleeting passage from past to future concerns. The purpose of meditation is to *freeze* time, mimicking eternity by squeezing the richness from the present moment. We cannot prepare for eternity unless we cultivate the habit of living, loving, and exhausting the present moment. That is what it means to live life in the light of eternity. That is what it means to be alive each moment.

The other accessible approach to eternity reflects humanity's universal sense of emptiness—the feeling that, in our present lives, what we have is neither all there is nor all we need. Although people tend to cram their lives with experience, at day's end many of them lament, "Is this all there is?" The poet Wordsworth yearned for a lost "splendor in the grass." Saint Augustine was persuaded that only God could fill human emptiness: "Our hearts are restless until they rest in thee." Wordsworth and the Mormons, as well as many who believe in past-life regression, believe not only that we are intended for more, but that we have in fact been snatched from a primordial Paradise and yearn to return home.

That Christians regard resurrection as fact rather than wishful thinking renders the univeral prospect of eternity less poignant. Theology, alas, is written in analytical prose, and not in the poetry it deserves. Yet resurrection is humankind's common aspiration. As the phoenix rose from the ashes of its own destruction, so we humans expect our spirits to rise in a new creation. In such an eternal state, intimacy will no longer be rare and reckless, but the standard for all relationships. Pain will pass. Disappointment will disappear. We will survive life's struggle, and love will last.

Inasmuch as death is inevitable, we humans owe it to ourselves to be farsighted and to look beyond it to our common future. The book you hold in your hands is not, unfortunately, a Michelin Guide to the afterlife. There are no road maps in the appendix, no recommendations for inns to seek out on your ultimate journey. Although heaven most definitely consists of many mansions, I cannot give you directions to the one with your name on it—or mine.

Nevertheless, there is much more than idle speculation in humanity's perennial expectation that the best is yet to be. As a Christian, I hold resurrection to be the cornerstone of my faith. As a student of human nature, I am struck by the near-universal conviction across all ages and cultures that the human spirit will not only survive death but prevail over it. Death is not the final frontier.

My shortcomings as the ultimate travel guide to the afterlife stem, in part, from the fact that I haven't as yet made the trip myself. But consider that the greatest voyagers in history also lacked detailed information about their destinations. Because they were prepared for inevitabilities and surprises, Alexander, Marco Polo, Columbus, Drake, Lewis and Clark, Livingstone, Burton, Amundsen, and Lindbergh were able to venture boldly without detailed knowledge. The great African and polar expeditions took years to assemble and involved not only provisioning but rigorous physical and mental training. America's space program made even more meticulous demands on our astronauts before they ventured into the void. Our first spaceman, Alan Shepard, trained two full years for a journey that lasted only fifteen minutes.

Death is inevitable, but eternity will take some getting used to. It only makes sense for us to prepare for our ultimate adventure by living our present lives in the light of eternity.

When Albert Einstein was asked what lay beyond infinity, he replied simply, "The face of God." Saint Paul conceded that in the present life we witness reality as in a distorting mirror, but he promised that in eternity we will see clearly. Despite our present lack of complete clarity, let us plan our inevitable journey now.

# ONE

# DEATH DOESN'T HURT—LIFE DOES

Death, where is thy sting?
1 CORINTHIANS 15:55

In her declining days, actress Katharine Hepburn spoke for the majority of mortals when she asked her friends:

Why is everyone so sad? I shan't be at all pleased if the last thing I see on this good earth are your sour expressions. Please cheer up. I've lived a long and magnificent life. . . . I'm ready to say my final goodbye, my dears. Sometimes as I drift off, I can see Spence [the late Spencer Tracy] walking on the beach, waiting for me, and I know soon that we will be together again. So don't under any circumstances feel sorry for me.

When Shakespeare's morbid Prince Hamlet posed his celebrated question—"To be, or not to be?"—he approached death as an equal option to life. Every healthy human instinct insists that Hamlet had it wrong—that life, however difficult, is infinitely preferable to oblivion. Faith and instinct alike are life affirming, maintaining that death is but a passage to transcendence—a brief curtain and dimming of lights before a magnificent and permanent final act. For the faithful, death marks neither an end nor even a beginning, but a continuation and consummation of all we have loved and learned in this life. All humanity aspires to a life free of pain and uncertainty. Few find it this side of eternity, but we can all prepare for it now.

☙

JOSEPH BERNARDIN sent his traditional thousands of Christmas cards earlier than usual in 1996, because he knew he was dying and might not last until the holidays. In fact he succumbed in mid-November, on his mother's ninety-second birthday, sixty-two years to the day after his father had died of the same dread disease—cancer.

More than many of us, the cardinal archbishop of Chicago was blessed by faith and buoyed by hope, and even privileged in the knowledge that his case was incurable. As it turned out, he had three months to prepare for what used to be called a "good death." Like many another person so stricken, he wondered, Why me? and, Why so soon? But he was determined to greet death not as an enemy but as a final friend that could conduct him home to eternal life with the God he had served for sixty-eight years.

Bernardin died as people used to die before antibiotics, chemotherapy, and expensive life-support systems—relatively quickly, surrounded by friends and family, and lucid to the end. I wish my own parents had been blessed with such good deaths, but each died alone in advanced age in an anonymous nursing home after years of pain, as well as physical and mental decline, having long since become only a shadow of the vital persons I remember as a child. For each, death was a release. It didn't hurt, but life had.

Sadly, modern medicine has managed to extend life without ensuring the quality of our final years. In times past, people died quickly of disease, infection, or injury while still in the prime of their lives. Today's longer life expectancy is marred by the anguish, loneliness, and incapacity of lingering illness for which death can only be deemed deliverance. In a recent poll the Kaiser Family Foundation revealed that fewer than one in four adult Americans admit to fearing death, but two-thirds of us are terrified by the prospect of our declining years.

When death was swift and faith was strong, sorrow was salved by hope. Surrounded by their loved ones, the dying could conceive of the resurrection of their bodies and the permanence of their spirits because they were in full possession of their faculties. But what of today's elderly, shuffled off to the solitude of nursing homes with deteriorating bodies and minds? Can they conceive of passing into eternal bliss in their condition? It is a heavy test of faith. But their hope has stood the test of time.

## The Perennial Hope

From the dawn of recorded history, people have cherished the hope that their spirits would survive death. Faith in an afterlife pervaded religion and philosophy alike. The hankering for eternity survives to this day, even among persons who possess little faith to support it. For example, Sir Arthur Conan Doyle, the cunning mastermind who created Sherlock Holmes, ardently sought to communicate with the soul of his dead son. In his quest he employed mediums, who failed him.

People who assume that *survival of the soul* is a fundamental Christian belief are gravely mistaken. In fact, Christian doctrine posits: *I believe in the resurrection of the body, and life everlasting.* The afterlife is for complete creatures, who exist in a new state of unimaginable satisfaction. (No wispy, disembodied spirits in the Christian heaven!)

Christians believe that Jesus became the firstborn of a new creation, inaugurating the kingdom of God, in which all persons, regardless of their faith traditions, are now citizens who enjoy the promise of new life. In eternity, we will be the same, yet different—just as Jesus was the same yet somehow different in his new life. We will be transformed.

At the time William Faulkner received the Nobel Prize for Literature, the world was threatened by nuclear annihilation. In his acceptance speech the author expressed his conviction that mankind would not only survive but prevail. In eternal terms, that is precisely the conviction of Christians, and it is based squarely on the victory of Jesus over death. Christ did not simply survive; he prevailed over death and, as a whole person—body and spirit—assumed new life.

### *Instinct for Survival*

The human instinct for survival cannot obscure the fact that the majority of lives on earth are nasty, brutish, and short. The pursuit of happiness, an enterprise invented by the Enlightenment, is indulged effectively only by the comfortable classes of the industrialized world. Even there, its successful pursuit is impeded by ignorance, violence, accidents, and ill health, and numbed by drugs, alcohol, sex, and therapies.

Experience suggests that cramming this life with pleasure is not only frivolous but foredoomed. By his own admission, the young Thomas Merton's proposed life of pleasure was cut short in Rome by an abscessed tooth. He found it impossible to be a sensualist while his teeth ached. He ended up a Trappist monk.

Having suffered reverses in our relentless attempt to pursue pleasure, those of us past oat-sowing age learn to husband our energies, cut our losses, moderate our expectations, choose safe occupations and reliable friends, and become philosophical. If we can also manage to avoid accidents and ill health, and cultivate a positive attitude, we may reach a level of contentment. Of course, we do immeasurably better in life if we have someone to love who loves us in return.

Death, ironically, is more predictable than life. For the person of faith, the eternal promise is more certain than what will happen tomorrow or even in the next hour. I do not know whom I will run into when I take a break from writing, but faith tells me that I will spend eternity with God if I am not foolish enough to be indifferent to him now.

It is understandable that we fear the process of dying, because it may involve pain or decrepitude and a waning of our faculties and senses. But even the fervent atheist conceives of death only as an end; it does not hurt. For the believer, death is both an end and a beginning—a curtain that drops only to rise on a new scene. In the theater the third act is when all the conflicts get resolved and the boy gets the girl. In *our* own final act, we get God.

## Cheating Death

Although living is arguably more problematical than dying, the universal human tendency is to prolong the former and postpone the latter. Modern medicine, while falling short of ensuring eternal life, has vastly extended Americans' life expectancy: from just fifty-four years in 1920 to more than seventy-five years today. Lamentably, Social Security is hard pressed to support these extra years on earth, and medicine cannot guarantee our quality of life during the reprieve.

Realizing that fact, some brave souls still in their vital years have decided to finance not just a long life but a resurrection for themselves. Paul Michaels, a vitamin salesman, and his wife, Maureen, are still in their forties; along with their teenage son, Alex, they are betting that science will restore their lives in the next century or so. According to Jonathan Leake of London's *Sunday Times,* their plan after death is to be bled, filled with antifreeze, packed in ice, flown to Detroit, and lowered into a vat of liquid nitrogen at minus 196 degrees centigrade in the expectation that scientists will soon devise a way of restoring them to life.

The Cryonic Institute in Detroit charges $35,000 per person for this service, payable through a life insurance policy costing about $100 a month. "I hope to achieve what man has only dreamed of until now: dying and taking it with me," Michaels comments. His wife predicts that "it'll be like emigrating, but instead of going to another country, we're going to the future."

To motivate future scientists to defrost their family, the Michaels have established a trust fund in Liechtenstein with the unusual provision that *they,* not their heirs, are to be the beneficiaries. Compound interest from investments, they reason, will provide a hedge against inflation and provide a nest egg for their future after they are revived.

The moment a death certificate is signed, a specially trained London mortician will cut into the Michaelses' jugular veins and carotid arteries, pumping a glycerine-based antifreeze into the arteries and draining blood from the veins. The antifreeze not only preserves the bodies, but prevents the breakage of extremities when they are frozen. Dr. Brian Grout, former secretary of the Society of Low Temperature Biology, confirms that while scientists have known for some time how to freeze and revive small clumps of cells, they have not yet revived anything as complex as a whole person.

Barry Albin-Dyer, the London mortician engaged to prepare the Michaelses for eventual resurrection, observes that they are unusual among his clients in wanting to be with one another in their next lives. More typical is the doctor who refused to talk to the

*Times* because he has not told his wife of his plans. "I think he's looking forward to eternity without her," Mr. Albin-Dyer says.

Opting for the deep freeze as a hedge against death does not address life's real dilemma, which is managing to get from one day to the next with a modicum of hope and satisfaction. In life-or-death situations, it is life that perplexes; by comparison, death is simple. That is why people of faith view life in the light of eternity—the bigger picture. When I told my wife about the Michaels family's bet on resurrection, she countered not with a scientific question ("What are their chances?") but with the practical one ("What's the advantage of returning to a strange world as old people with infirmities and no friends?"). Grasping at life with so little satisfaction in store falls lamentably short of what people of faith believe God has prepared for those who love him.

I am inclined to believe the scarcity of serious literature on the afterlife reflects the Creator's intention to focus his revelation (and our attention) on everyday living, where we have a daily opportunity to make choices. In eternity, God will choose for us. For Christians, Jews, and Moslems, revelation begins with the book of Genesis. Eden provides the first clue to God's original intentions and suggests why life this side of eternity falls so short of expectation. With the loss of Eden, death entered the world, and life became toil. It's worth revisiting the garden and our first parents to see what there is to learn about the Paradise we lost and hope to regain eternally.

## The Trouble with Paradise

Paradise illustrates what the world once was and might still be were it not for the perversity of human nature. Even before the advent of Adam and Eve, the twin sins of pride and envy had set the universe at odds with its Creator. The tempter in the garden, disguised as a snake, had already yielded to ambition himself and had fallen short of the divinity he sought. In Eden, the snake held out to the first man and woman a promise of independence and god-likeness, which he already knew to be a lie. The story of the Fall therefore begins with sham and malevolence.

In Milton's *Paradise Lost,* the first human pair do not appear until the story is well under-way: in a kind of second act, following the uprising and fall of the angels, whose revolt did not spoil heaven but "created" hell. (Indeed, there is no reason to believe that *God* created hell at all. Hell is only solitude and alienation and emptiness; Milton called it "chaos." Philosophers define evil as *nothing*—literally the absence of being. By that definition, hell is the utter absence of anything good. It is the fruit of Satan's thwarted ambition.)

Paradise *was* destroyed by the human sin of pride. Man and woman, created in God's image, made themselves God's enemies. Paradise, their eternal home, was not only lost: it utterly ceased to exist.

The skeptical reader may have sufficient difficulty acknowledging the existence of Adam and Eve without dragging Lucifer and the angels into the story. Why, you may ask, can't we simply find a moral to the myth without dragging additional characters and subplots onto the stage? Why not be scholarly and trace the Genesis story to its Babylonian roots, thereby lending a patina of respectability to the account, rather than ramble on about snakes and forbidden fruit?

My response is that I trust the intelligence of my reader to distinguish between history and imagination. However mythical, Genesis is God's story to tell and has a moral to convey. Fairy tales are no less true for being fanciful. A newspaper account is only paper and ink, but wisdom sometimes comes in fancy wrappers, as here. What we are seeking is an explanation of why life is so difficult, why death is inevitable, and why life may prevail after death.

At the outset of the Bible, we are assured that God alone made the world and that he made it *good*—not simply that he made it *well*. The distinction is crucial. We know God himself is good, but we are tempted to make unwarranted excuses about the world. God created the world from nothing, ensuring that all creation is dependent entirely upon him and finds its purpose and fulfillment in him.

Precisely because we are God's, we are good. We are his idea come to life—not transient creatures to be cast off, but intended for eternity. But when evil enters the world, it brings death. Paradise is lost when man and woman no longer acknowledge their Creator, thereby losing the idea of themselves.

But the Paradise we lost was not itself perfect. As the *Catechism of the Catholic Church* suggests, "The universe was created 'in a state of journeying' . . . toward an ultimate perfection yet to be attained, to which God has destined it" (#302). Even from the outset, Paradise was not to be our final fulfillment. We were intended to work our way to eternity, day by day. Lamentably, with Paradise lost, the journey would be harder and death would mark the boundary between time and eternity. But death need not be feared; it is how we handle life that determines the kind of eternity to which we can realistically aspire.

That's a thought to take into eternity and to start applying now.

## *"The Devil Made Me Do It"*

Imaginative children devoutly long for a fairy godmother to be their personal protector and wish fulfiller, but in time they reluctantly consign fairies and genies to fiction, along with Santa Claus and the Easter Bunny. Angels have greater staying power with adults. There is, in fact, a strong Christian tradition that we each possess a guardian angel—a spirit creature assigned to us from infancy to death to protect and direct us and to care and intercede for us. Saint Basil affirmed, "Beside each believer stands an angel as protector and shepherd leading him to life."

Skeptics, while open to the existence of life-forms on other planets, may nevertheless balk at acknowledging angels—especially the one that is permanently assigned to look over their shoulders. The book of Revelation, however, is clear about these spirits. They are not fanciful but useful, and judging from their frequent appearance in scripture, they enjoy full employment. Saint Augustine, incidentally, notes that "angel" is not really their name but their profession (just as a man may be called a plumber because that is what he does, but not who he is). Angels are spirits who often act as messengers. As a young man, I studied intertestamental history with the late Cardinal Jean Daniélou in Paris, plumbing the silent centuries between the close of the Old Testament revelation and the beginning of the New. This was, of course, the era in which Jesus appeared. To the Jews' way of thinking, theirs was a world populated not only by men and women but also by angels.

I do not refer here to guardian angels alone, but to cherubim and seraphim, powers and dominions, archangels, and every rank of spirit populating the heavens in a hierarchy more complex than *Burke's Peerage*. To the Jews of Jesus' time, this spirit world was real and almost palpable. God indeed was in his heaven, but he enjoyed a great deal of company. When a courier was sent to announce the conception of the Savior to his intended mother, it was only natural that an angel be the messenger—and that an angelic host proclaim Jesus' birth in Bethlehem.

We know from his diabolical works that Lucifer, the fallen angel who posed as a snake in Eden, was no good at all. But what possible good are all these other angelic spirits, who not only pre-date man but live in eternity? It is enough to note that they are useful because they have work to do. Of those angels named in the Bible, for example, Michael occupied himself battling Lucifer, and Gabriel brought news of the Savior. My wife insists that she wants no part of an eternity consisting of passive contemplation but hopes to accomplish something and to be helpful in heaven. Since this is what angels already do in eternity, it seems she will have her way.

In his *Man and Superman,* George Bernard Shaw fancied a heaven in which the blessed still strive for accomplishment, while the damned are content to worship their own images and to wallow in hell as in a luxury resort. We can agree with Shaw that those who invest in something beyond themselves (the saved) will have something to do in eternity, whereas the self-indulgent (the damned) will have nothing to do. In fact, that's a powerful thought to take into eternity.

But even the evil angels occupy themselves in eternity, and Lucifer himself took on the successful seduction of our Adam and Eve. Ever since, generations of men and women have been tempted to pardon their own perversities by insisting that the devil made them do it.

### The Knowledge of Good and Evil

In more prudish and prurient times, the association of nakedness and shame in the account of Adam and Eve's fall from grace prompted commentators to equate the forbidden fruit with sex. But the biblical narrative does not support that interpretation. So long as man and woman walked with God in the garden, they were not even aware that they were naked. Adam and Eve were content with God and with each other; their Eden was the original Peaceable Kingdom, wherein every creature looked to man as his master who would do it no harm. There were no threatening beasts in the garden because no animal (including man) acted beastly; beastliness and inhumanity came only after the Fall.

Nakedness is meaningless unless there is something to hide. After their treason, Adam and Eve attempted not just to cover themselves but to hide altogether from their Creator. As regards the other creatures in the garden, God had given Adam and Eve roles as their conservators and guardians. Here is the charming passage in which God presents each species to Adam to receive its name: "So out of the ground the Lord God formed every beast of the field and every bird of the air, and brought them to the man to see what he would call them; and whatever the man called every living creature, that was its name" (Genesis 2:19).

Nowadays, when we name a newborn child or a kitten or a puppy, we mimic Adam's original dominion over creation. However, things are not quite the same now as in Eden before the Fall. On occasion, my Scottish terrier bites me, and my cats bare their claws when I attempt to be masterful. After the loss of Eden, few humans attempt to domesticate a gorilla or a crocodile. What is dramatic about Adam and Eve's banishment from Paradise is not so much that they had to leave a lovely garden as that they were *different* after their transgression and no longer suited to the place.

Paradise, for all its apparent beauty and creature comforts, was not a place for loafing. Adam and Eve tilled the garden, but they did so contentedly. What truly distinguished Paradise was not the scenery but the composure of its inhabitants. Man and woman were satisfied and at peace with God, with each other, and with every creature in the garden. Of more importance, they were at peace within themselves. Now, by contrast, we characterize people by their contradictions and complexities, their perversities and inconsistencies, and their utter unpredictability. By current standards of sophistication, Adam and Eve appear simple, but they were "together" as no mere mortals have been ever since, and love was their only motive—until they wanted more.

## The Subtle Serpent

Like every fairy tale since, the drama of the Fall rests on a challenge—in the case of Adam and Eve, something they were forbidden to do. The great Christian essayist G. K. Chesterton explained in *Orthodoxy* that

> the true citizen of fairyland is obeying something that he does not understand at all. In the fairy tale an incomprehensible happiness rests upon an incomprehensible condition. A box is opened, and all evils fly out. A word is forgotten, and cities perish. A lamp is lit, and love flies away. A flower is plucked, and human lives are forfeited. An apple is eaten, and the hope of God is gone.

To appreciate the magnitude of Adam's sin of pride, we must resist thinking of him as a calculating adult like ourselves, with a long childhood of schooling and parental guidance behind him. According to Genesis, Adam was created as a full-blown adult, yet no creature since can have been more childlike than this utterly unique creature who was dust one moment and a solitary, sentient, thinking animal the next. The only word that conveys the first man's feelings is "astonishment"—what Chesterton called "elementary wonder":

> When we are very young, children do not need fairy tales: we only need tales. Mere life is interesting enough. A child

of seven is excited by being told that Tommy opened a door and saw a dragon. But a child of three is excited by being told that Tommy opened a door.

By the measure of wonder, Adam, however mature in physical stature, was a child. Paradise was not the primary source of his astonishment; his very existence was bewildering and romantic. How, then, could this infantile man possibly sin? What could be his motive, and how could God take his transgression so seriously that it made life onerous and death inevitable ever since?

Chesterton was himself so childlike as an adult that he would get lost in familiar London streets and phone his wife to ask where he was. He defended his bewilderment by asserting that most men were more permanently lost than he because they had forgotten *what* they are. He, by contrast, never lost his sense of wonder.

If we could get into Adam's head, we would find uncalculating wonderment. So, how did he manage to spoil humankind's excellent adventure for himself and us? By failing a test. The test of all happiness is gratitude, Chesterton affirms, adding that as a happy, young, and skeptical adult, he himself felt grateful for life's blessings but did not know whom to thank.

Here Adam enjoyed an enormous advantage. He knew personally the source of his happiness, for God walked with him in the Paradise created expressly for him. Adam was the beneficiary of literally everything: Eden and its benign creatures, a woman to love, and the very gift of life, with the wonder of mind, the pleasure of sensation, and the excitement of anticipation. The blind poet Milton, describing the very stars above Paradise, called them sapphires. These heavenly jewels belonged to just one man. In the face of all this largesse, Adam did an extraordinarily childish thing and, with Eve, demanded more.

It is a sentimental fact that, in the twentieth century, we have

persuaded ourselves, against all evidence, that children are inno-
cents. This attitude is surely an improvement over earlier centuries, when children were considered beastly and treated brutally.
But our current sentimentality about children, while humane in
intent, flies in the face of the facts. Children, however charming,
are often perverse, selfish, and destructive—not to mention ungrateful. When we accuse other adults of being childish, we are affirming this very thing—not that they are wicked but that, like
children, they are irresponsible and self-centered, destroying
rather than building, and leaving a mess for others to clean up. If
you persist in believing children to be innocent and civilized, then
you obviously have not met a child in the aisles and checkout
counters of a supermarket.

Paradise was based on responsibility. It was irresponsibility
that lost Eden, transformed everyday living into the trial it is, and
placed eternity on the far side of death. We must now die to this
world in order to live in the next.

## The Man Who Had Everything

Every Christmas season, merchants are challenged to suggest to
shoppers what to buy for "the man who has everything." But what
about a child who has everything? Children always want something more. To return to the first man-child, Adam: what could he
possibly want that he had not been given by God in Paradise?
What every child wants: to have its own way, to rebel against its
dependency, to smash things to show his power, to throw a
tantrum, to play master of the universe. Lucifer, the angel who had
already thrown his own tantrum, appealed to Adam and Eve as to
spoiled children. Of the fruit of the tree of knowledge of good and
evil, the serpent promised: "God knows that when you eat of it
your eyes will be opened, and you will be like God" (Genesis 3:5).

In the course of history, there have been countless attempts to recreate Paradise. Some utopias (like Thomas More's) never got off the printed page, but many others were actually created in America, from New Harmony to Oneida, Brook Farm, Nauvoo, Amana, and the Shakertowns of the last century to the communes and ashrams of the 1960s. What is remarkable about every attempted utopia is that each, like Eden, has prohibitions. Every ideal community is conceived to exalt mankind's better nature and organized to minimize his worst. Ironically, experiments in recreating Paradise on earth seek to free the spirit but are riddled with rules to enable the community to function in the face of anarchic human nature. Utopias occasionally succeed, but at the cost of totalitarian tyranny: revolutionary France, Puritan New England, the Stalinist Soviet Union. They more often fail for the same reason that Paradise was lost—because their members choose not to follow the rules.

## Don't Blame the Woman

Misogynists have been quick to blame the woman for the Fall by noting Adam's initial reluctance to disobey God. But the fact is that both were in on it together, and Adam preferred his wife's opinion to God's. When discovered, both of them ducked and dodged and blamed the snake and each other. The nakedness to which their eyes were opened was their embarrassment.

Was the original sin so awful as to forfeit Paradise not only for Adam and Eve but for the rest of humankind as well? The catechism insists that Adam can be understood only in the light of Christ, and the gravity of Adam's sin appreciated only by reference to the extraordinary measures God took to redeem the sons and daughters of Adam. Christians believe that God sent his Son to become the "new Adam"—to walk not in an Eden but on the barren hills of Galilee, and at length to suffer and die for love of the creatures who had betrayed his Father.

The original sin has been variously characterized as pride, envy, covetousness, and ambition; its motive was childish and perverse. The expulsion of humankind from Paradise was the first instance of "tough love." Traditional pedagogues insist that an adult cannot reason or bargain with a spoiled child; one must punish him for his own good and hope he will mature into an adult. So God treated Adam and Eve. Paradise was lost, but God ensured that man would ultimately prevail. Whereas Adam the man-child was irresponsible, at length a God-man—Jesus Christ —would be responsible even unto death, meriting something infinitely better than Eden. Now we would all be heirs of heaven. For the children of Adam and Eve life would hurt, but Christ's death would restore an eternal Paradise for those who learn the responsibility of love.

"This very day," Jesus promised the dying thief, "you will be with me in Paradise."

## Living in the Light of Eternity

Death doesn't hurt—life does. Still, no one prizes death; rather, we cling to life. Death is nothing; life is everything. Every religious tradition affirms that although we are prone to suffering in our present incarnation, future life holds greater expectations. But only on condition that we embrace life now, committing ourselves to it fully, rather than taking life for granted. Hell is for drifters— those who in the midst of life are already dead—whereas for those who affirm life, celebrate it, and respect every living thing, theirs is the kingdom of heaven.

Adam, the man-child, chose himself over the source of his life. He ate the forbidden fruit because he demanded that life ensure him a free lunch. Adam was not only foolish but irresponsible.

Our Creator charges us, as he did Adam, to embrace life as a gift, to love the living, and to tend the earth as God's garden.

Christians recognize Jesus as the new Adam. Even in death, Jesus was wholly responsible to life and restored its original promise of eternity. Today is not only the first day of the rest of our lives; it is our investment in eternity. Religious traditions agree: as we live now, we will live forever.

Walt Kelly's Pogo once proclaimed famously, "We have met the enemy, and he is us." There are but two approaches to living: to look upon it as an endless series of trials to be overcome, or as an adventure full of promise. The facts of life support either interpretation; but if we choose to shrink from life, it is because *we* are the problem. Eternity is but the extension of living, and its fulfillment. By embracing life, we bless it and its Creator, and we open ourselves to new life.

English playwright Alan Bennett recalls the sage instruction of a judge to a hung jury. Exasperated, the jury's foreman demanded of the judge, "When must we come to a verdict?"

"When you are too tired to go on," replied the judge.

Unfortunately, that is advice we cannot afford to take. We will never choose life if we wait until we are weary with indecision. Eternity hangs in the balance. We must decide now to live in its light.

# TWO

# YOU ARE NOT
# THE FIRST PERSON
# TO MAKE THIS TRIP

Eternal life is beyond past, present and
future: we come from it, we live in its
presence, we return to it.

PAUL TILLICH,
THE ETERNAL NOW

As we approach the autumn of our lives, our sense of
mortality can become more acute and our isolation
more palpable. Many of my retired friends turn first to the
obituaries in the morning paper for the news that affects
them most. Which of their friends and associates, they wonder, has departed this mortal coil, leaving them behind, more
alone, more isolated in life as a minority of one?

Of course, everyone faces death alone and unexperi-
enced. Of course, we are loathe to leave our loved ones. And
of course, we fear the pain that might accompany an illness
leading to death. But death itself need not be feared. Each of
us has faced every major challenge in life in the same way—
for the first time, with no experience, and with some trepida-
tion. But we passed each milestone fully realizing that

billions of other men and women before us had confronted the same rites of passage and prevailed.

So with death. The vast majority of Americans have faith that it is not life's end but marks a new beginning that will have no end. We do not know precisely what to expect, but we do know that all of humankind make the same journey. The 5.6 billion men, women, and children who share life on earth with you and me at the moment are but a tiny minority of all who have lived before us or will be born after our departure. When you and I pass from this life we will not be alone. We will be joining the majority.

ᚫ

MANY FEAR that their final journey will be a lonely one. After all, one dies alone. But we have already experienced that we are each alone throughout our lives, imprisoned within the solitude of our thoughts and emotions, experiencing agonies and ecstasies that cannot be shared but only suggested to others. We spend much of our energy in life denying this solitude—distracting ourselves with activities or daydreams, preferring short to long thoughts and sensation to thinking at all. "Be still and know that I am God," the psalmist counsels. But since contemplation more often than not reminds us of our solitude, we are inclined to put it off.

Death, alas, is not worth pondering, but our future is. Death brings completion, not dissolution. Nevertheless, few persons seek their own demise until this life becomes intolerable. Martyrs die not by choice, but that others might live; their courage is life affirming and nourished by hope. Most of us are not so brave. However tenuous our present lives may be, we cling to them, partly from instinct, partly from reason: "Better the devil we know . . ."

The only real sorrow in death is felt by those who are left behind. Your own death will be an opening into life, but when friends and loved ones die they take a part of your life with them. All the more reason not to fear following them, but to look forward to sharing the liberation they have already achieved.

You need not be religious to agree that death and taxes are sure things. But after a lifetime of paying one's debts, everyone meets his maker. Death marks the end of debts and the beginning of dividends. It means joining the majority.

## The Silence of Lazarus

Lazarus was the brother of Martha and Mary—all three of them among Jesus' closest friends. Shortly before Jesus' own death, Lazarus died of unexplained causes, and was four days in the tomb before Jesus arrived at their home in Bethany to pay respects to the survivors. Seeing the grave, Jesus wept—the only recorded display of such emotion. "See how he loved him," witnesses marveled.

Lazarus was truly and long dead, wrapped mummylike in the Jewish fashion and buried (as Jesus would soon be) in a cave sealed with a great stone at its mouth. Proclaiming himself the resurrection and the life, Jesus went out to the tomb with the intention of restoring Lazarus to life. Martha, although she was careful to affirm Jesus' power over life and death, sought to deter him, objecting that her brother's body was already decomposing. "Lord, he stinketh!" she said—providing the one line from the Bible memorized by every Sunday school child, who delights in hurling it at his companions.

Turning aside Martha's objection, Jesus called out to Lazarus, who promptly emerged from his tomb still wrapped head to foot in his burial cloths. Lazarus, clearly dead as a doornail, found himself restored to life. At this juncture any first-time reader of the

New Testament might expect that the formerly dead man, after expressing gratitude, would report on his experience, revealing what you and I can expect on the other side of death. Yet Lazarus said nothing about it. His silence was deafening.

If Jesus' friend failed to report on his experience of the afterlife, is it because nothing can be said? Not according to public opinion. More than a decade ago pollster George Gallup Jr. revealed that 23 million living Americans had undergone near-death trauma before recovering; unlike Lazarus, they had plenty to say about it. Eight million of them reported "mystical" experiences beyond life. They are convinced that they have already made the ultimate journey on a trial basis.

Predictably, those who claim to have experienced a temporary taste of eternity describe the afterlife in terms that fit their religious and cultural predilections. But that does not necessarily reduce heaven to fabrication or wish fulfillment. If we are to accept Jesus' word that there are "many mansions," and to make sense of Saint Paul's reference to a "third heaven" (implying a first and second), then it is reasonable to assume that eternity is not a totalitarian state of standardized bliss but is uniquely suited to each of us. Just as your life is different from mine, so too will our eternities be different from each other's. The only thing likely to be the same for everyone in the afterlife is the presence of God—or the fearful alternative of his eternal *absence,* which we call hell.

To comprehend heaven, we must first make a detour to hell.

### *A Lonely Detour*

The story of Adam and Eve might have ended with their sin and expulsion from Paradise; but according to Genesis, such was God's graciousness and confidence in his flawed creatures that he consigned man, woman, and their progeny not to hell, but to what we call *real life:* to pain and pleasure, labor and recreation, purpose and accident, sickness and health, hatred and love, regret and occasional enchantment—and in the end, decline and death. But if real life is not quite Paradise, it is surely not hell.

Expelled from Paradise into the real world, alienated from their Creator but still under his care, Adam's progeny had a second chance: to continue to choose themselves, or to reconsider their sin and choose their Creator—that is, to decide between hell and heaven. At length, God made it easier for humankind by sending his Son to mend the original breach and to open heaven to the sons and daughters of Adam and Eve. Paradise was never restored, but we were graced and invested with God's Spirit, inheriting an intimacy with God that even our first parents did not enjoy. In place of Eden, we are presented with a new creation—a new heaven and a new earth. Of course, this is all a matter of faith; our actual experience is limited to life here, east of Eden, where we can work out our eternity.

Hell is not God's creation. Satan and his angels made it for themselves. Lucifer is not satisfied with hell, but given a second chance, he still would not opt for heaven. It was his original home but not to his taste—too much God and not enough of himself. Whatever else hell is, it is the eternal choice by the creature of himself over his Creator. God does not condemn anyone to hell; creatures write the ticket themselves.

## Hopelessness

Why would anyone choose hell? At hell's portal, Dante in his *Divine Comedy* posted a sign that reads, "Abandon all hope, you who enter here." It is the poet's vision of the inferno that has captured the imagination of Christians and unbelievers alike ever since. Hell for Dante is a place of torment, but the agony is essentially spiritual: hell is the home of the hopeless.

Traditionally, Christianity has assumed suicides to have damned themselves, because one who takes his own life has abandoned hope and therefore God, its source. Disregarding any religious dimension, self-destruction is mankind's supreme expression of solitude and alienation. The suicide says, in effect, "Life is a cheat and I can depend on no one but myself; since I cannot find satisfaction, it is better to have nothing. I choose oblivion."

Society considers suicide sick and even criminal behavior, but many people will admit to having considered it, dispassionately, at some particularly trying stage in their lives. "To sleep, perchance to dream," Hamlet mused as he contemplated the attractiveness of taking fate into his own hands rather than allowing fate to have its way with him. In his *Poor Richard's Almanac* Benjamin Franklin estimated that "nine men in ten are suicides," abbreviating their lives by irresponsibility, or by acquiescence, or by design. If people truly prized their lives, Franklin reflected, they would live more sensibly.

We had best bracket the wish of the terminally ill to die: if the spirit is gone and replaced by animal agony, the decision is driven not by an absence of hope but by a surfeit of pain. My own mother and aunt both endured protracted death agonies in advanced age, and effectively chose death—not by calling on the Hemlock Society, but by refusing nourishment. Both were spirited women; what remained of their spirits did not abandon hope in their Redeemer but only loosened the grip on the dregs of life that were all that remained to them.

### Punishment

Can you imagine anyone actually choosing damnation? Dante's truly frightful depiction of hell exemplifies a consistent theme:

everyone there elects to be damned, and is locked into an eternal round of pursuing the same miserable fancies that consumed him or her in life. Consider the two lovers Paolo and Francesca: they consummated their unholy passion on earth; now in death Dante depicts them locked eternally in an embrace they cannot break. They are bound to each other like glue.

You get the idea. We know that Dante introduced real people into his allegorical inferno to frighten the living into virtue, but his underlying moral was that the eternal punishment for sin is its endless pursuit. The reason hell is such a miserable, unruly place is that everyone there is both self-absorbed and peevishly—even hopelessly—dissatisfied, doomed to endlessly repeat the same behavior that was his undoing in life.

For all we know there may be hellfire, but then again this may only be a metaphor for burning ambition or envy or lust—or cold indifference. We are forever getting our fingers burned in this life; if we learn from the experience, there is no need to burn in hell. As heaven has many mansions, Dante's hell has many levels, each dedicated to similar sins, each with its own appropriate punishment. But what of the multitude at hell's gate who mill about aimlessly, denied entry both to heaven and to hell? Dante says they are the indifferent: those who never made up their minds or made a hard choice in their lives, committing themselves to no one and nothing, endlessly straddling life's fence, walking away from love and commitment. In life they chose nothing, so nothing is their eternal reward.

A Christian hell that consists of eternally killing time in the pursuit of lost causes contrasts markedly with the Islamic inferno described in the Koran. Just as Muhammad's heaven is a sensuous garden of delights, his hell is characterized by physical torment. A fiery furnace burns the flesh without consuming it. His damned drink boiling water mixed with pus and eat the bitter fruit of a tree whose branches are devils' heads. In other references, however, the Prophet dispenses with these physical horrors to define hell as an anarchy of souls pursuing their own selfish ends without satisfaction.

If you have been content to believe all along in actual hellfire, you may accuse me of revisionism, but such is not my intention. Whatever hell is like, its true horror is the absence of God. If such a hell does not seem so very awful to selfish people, the horror is that they fail to comprehend what the damned have been denied. They risk missing it themselves through inadvertence and inattention in this life. As you consider that you are not the first to make the trip to eternity, you may wish to refocus your own life on eternal values—on love and truth, on beauty and responsibility. Hell is for people who think only in the short term.

## *Hell's History*

Although hell is not mentioned in the earliest Christian creeds, the Synod of Constantinople in 543 referred to it, and the Fourth Lateran Council in 1215 asserted that "some will receive perpetual punishment with the devil and the others everlasting glory with Christ." The Council of Florence in 1442 assumed vast numbers of people would be damned:

> The Holy Roman Church . . . firmly believes, professes, and proclaims that none of those outside the Catholic Church, not Jews, nor heretics, nor schismatics, can participate in eternal life, but will go into the eternal fire prepared for the devil and his angels unless they are brought into [the Catholic Church] before the end of life.

At the time of the council there was no Christian alternative to being Catholic, but mere church membership carried no guarantee of heaven. Pope Benedict XII in his constitution *Benedictus Deus* (1336) said, "We define that according to the general disposition of God the souls of those who die in actual mortal sin go down immediately after death into hell and are there tormented by the pains of hell." In modern times, without really addressing (let alone contradicting) its traditional teaching on hell, the Catholic Church's reforming Second Vatican Council in its *Constitution on the Church* (1964) declared that even atheists in good faith are eligible for salvation. Ironically, the dreaded Inquisition had a compassionate intent that reflected the prevailing fear of hell: better to torture the Jew or heretic into faith and help them to achieve repentance now than to consign them to the eternal torments of hell!

## Jesus and Hell

In his book *Eternal Life?* Catholic theologian Hans Küng notes that Jesus was not a hellfire-and-brimstone preacher: "Nowhere does he show any direct interest in hell. Nowhere does he describe the act of damnation or the torments of the damned." Oddly enough, it was an apocryphal book of the second century, the Apocalypse of Peter (subsequently rejected for inclusion in the New Testament), that persuaded the early church of hell's physical torments. It would be another millennium before Dante would pick up the theme, refine, and exploit it.

In Jesus' time, the prevailing Jewish concept of Sheol as a resting place for the dead was already changing. Traditionally, it had been depicted as a place of shadows and suspended animation where both the good and the evil were treated indiscriminately. Before the New Testament was written, however, Judaism had begun to make distinctions. Sheol now was reconceived as a place of rest and peace for the good awaiting the Messiah, while a new name, Gehenna, depicted a place of temporary punishment for the wicked, to become permanent after the last judgment. Inasmuch as the Jews assumed the underworld to be permanently dark, it is ironic that it could also be a place of eternal flames, but no one at the time seemed to mind the contradiction.

Jesus, on the other hand, never dwells on hell. His intention is not to threaten but to deliver the good news of salvation and the dawning of the kingdom of God. He challenges mankind to decide (in Küng's words) "for or against selfishness, for or against God, and therefore for salvation or perdition." The imperative is *conversion:* we must "turn around," from ourselves to God, in faith. Hell cannot compete with heaven, because it has no power to attract. Still, heaven must be chosen; it cannot be left to chance. Hell is for drifters, the self-indulgent, and the uncommitted.

## *The Demonic*

The Jews of Jesus' time, no less than the pagans, believed the world to be populated by demonic powers, which they feared. Just as there were hierarchies of angels eager to do God's bidding, it was assumed there were legions of personal demons to serve evil purposes. In spoofs of temptation we sometimes depict hapless mortals with an angel perched on one shoulder, a devil on the other, tugging their victims between virtue and vice. Humor aside, the ancients felt threatened by personal demons even before they came to believe in guardian angels. Before he embarked on his public life, Jesus himself was tempted in the desert by Satan himself.

Jesus not only miraculously fed the hungry and cured the sick; he ridded them of demons. To the present day, some mainstream Christian churches practice exorcism not only in extraordinary cases of supposed possession but as part of the traditional baptismal rite of initiation into the faith. Ritual exorcism proclaims that no one and nothing has the power to harm those whom God's Son died to save.

Not surprisingly, some of the most revealing portraits of hell come from the pens of unbelievers, since they simply expand on the hellish aspects of everyday life. In his play *No Exit,* Jean-Paul Sartre depicted hell as a barren room in which three flawed characters are condemned to endure one another's company eternally without privacy. Each inmate whines and attempts to manipulate the other, but no one gains an advantage. Nothing changes. Each seeks sympathy from the others for his or her own failings, but all are too self-absorbed to think of anyone else. It is easy to conclude that "hell is other people," but it is clear that each character is a self-contained misery: hell is ultimately oneself.

More lightheartedly, George Bernard Shaw depicted hell in a comic playlet, *Don Juan in Hell,* which demonstrated the playwright's tough-minded notions about how you and I might lift ourselves from our twin miseries of body and spirit. Religiously, the play's value consists in dramatizing convincingly how each individual chooses his own eternal fate. Shaw's Satan cynically exclaims:

> Written over the gate here are the words "Leave every hope behind, ye who enter." Only think what a relief that is! For what is hope? A form of moral responsibility. Here there is no hope, and consequently no duty, no work, nothing to be gained by praying, nothing to be lost by doing what you like. Hell, in short, is a place where you have nothing to do but amuse yourself.

In short, the damned are self-satisfied. They have damned themselves. But salvation is possible for those who seek it. The

frontier between hell and heaven, Shaw insists, "is only the difference between two ways of looking at things. Any road will take
you across if you really want to get there."

Audiences realized that Shaw's play was not really about the afterlife but about life's choices. For people of faith it amounts to the
same thing: God confirms one's choices eternally. Alarmingly, we
get what we want. Shaw observed the leisure classes of Edwardian
England blithely pursuing power and pleasure, just as Dante had
witnessed the mercenaries, princes, and voluptuaries of thir-
teenth-century Italy on the make. Both writers created hells for
their contemporaries that are no more or less than eternal exten-
sions of the lives they pursued on earth.

If these literary hells do not seem so horrible, it is because the
single-minded pursuit of pleasure and power at least yields something short-term, whereas the pursuit of lasting values may not
guarantee eternity. In this scenario, people of faith trust the Creator to understand his creatures better than they understand
themselves. In any event, our ultimate satisfaction probably defies
analysis.

### Revisionism and Mythology

Shaw conceived of a hell in which shallow people display their
fashions. There are fashions in theology as well. A generation ago
a book on this topic would not have been taken seriously. At that
time, revisionists debunked biblical mythology, substituted situ-
ational ethics for morality, reduced religion to mere "ultimate
concern," and replaced the personal God of Abraham with an impersonal Ground of Being. That comparatively recent take on revelation, while sophisticated and well intentioned, was interpreted
by believers and skeptics alike as the death knell of religion. Mag-
azines in the sixties produced cover stories proclaiming the death

of God, and serious commentators began to refer to our times as post-Christian.

A generation later, it is fashionable once again not only to focus on the truth underlying traditional religious myths but to conjure new and fanciful spiritual worlds nowhere revealed in Holy Writ. Whereas the challenge thirty years ago was to deny any reality behind the traditional accounts of Eden, heaven, hell, and a transcendent Deity, today our challenge is to extract from those myths essentially what is being revealed by God.

Human freedom requires people to make choices between good and evil and between their short-term and long-term interests. Because we are from the instant of birth presented with our own existence as a gift, we know that God rewards us; similarly we know from experience that people wittingly and unwittingly punish themselves and one another. The challenge is to serve ourselves and one another as God would do, cherishing values worth taking beyond this brief life. That requires decision.

For people of faith, the ultimate reality is that this life is but a prelude to the next, and that all life—here and beyond—is sustained by the Creator's love for his creatures. Hell is the denial of that reality. Hell is to choose to be permanently earthbound, locked within one's fragile ego, eternally alone.

You are not the first person to make this trip, which can be postponed but not avoided. Happily, we control our destinies by our choices. If we drift in life, we will drift eternally, like the souls at the gates of Dante's hell. Heaven is for the committed. We choose heaven by celebrating creation, by honoring our affections, by living responsibly, and by gratitude.

# THREE

# YOU *CAN* TAKE IT WITH YOU

I wear the chain I forged in life.

CHARLES DICKENS,
*A CHRISTMAS CAROL*

When the American frontier was still wild, an anonymous prospector scratched this final lament on the wall of his shack in Deadwood, South Dakota:

I lost my gun. I lost my horse. I'm out of food. The Indians are after me. But I've got all the gold I can carry.

Most moderns, when confronted with their own mortality, sense a kinship with the miner. As we approach and pass the September of our lives, we fear that all we have fought for and won will ultimately be stripped away. We must leave our gold behind.

But what if death has no dominion? Suppose that death is not a period, but merely a comma that marks a pause in our progress from this life to the next? What if the life we know is but a prelude to eternity? Then nothing we have achieved in this life can be lost but will be the gold we carry to the next.

**In fact, throughout history and across all cultures the vast majority of humankind has held that this life is not the end of living, and that we *can* take it with us—not fool's gold but the wealth of affection, experience, and knowledge we have accumulated in this life.**

ॐ

YOUR CAR, your furniture, and your stamp collection will not survive the journey from time to eternity, but your personality, character, intellect, culture, memories, curiosity, generosity, and affections are completely portable. They are already packed, ready to clear customs and cross the border. Christians believe that we will rise as Jesus did—intact as complete human beings, not just floating spirits. I am reconciled to being bald and freckled in eternity just as I am in time. The alternative—to be disembodied—would involve being *less* in the afterlife than we are in this one. It would suggest that God made a mistake in the first instance, that he should have made us angels, not complete women and men. That flesh and spirit are often in conflict in this life is no indictment of the physical. Our bodies give us joys as well as complaints. The original sin that caused the conflict—pride—was spiritual, not physical.

On balance, the indulgence of our senses is more natural than the dietary and exercise regimens we inflict on our bodies and the annoyance we feel when they fail to make us look as good and perform as well as we wish. We worry about our appearance, starve off pudgy pounds, bewail our ailments, and curse the aging process. I'm not the man or woman I used to be, we complain, as though we are less for no longer being twenty.

Christians have a loftier notion of flesh and blood. Saint Paul called our bodies temples of the Holy Spirit. One does not simply camp out in a temple. Our bodies are not just temporary tents for the soul, to be collapsed when we move on. They are permanent and deserve respect. As creatures beloved by our Creator, we are as much our bodies as our souls.

Unless I miss my guess, our trip into eternity will be remarkably like travel on earth. We will perforce travel light but will carry all our necessities, which, after all, are internal to us—built in, you might say. We will be whole, and our eyes and other senses will be open to wonder and enjoyment. We will not be puritans. Like all wise travelers, we will want to prepare so that our trip will balance reassurance with surprise.

## *The Reality of Resurrection*

Resurrection from death to life, far from being a pious hope, is in fact the center and foundation of Christianity. "If Christ did not rise, your faith is futile," Paul wrote to the Corinthians even before the evangelists wrote their gospels. "Truly, if our hope in Christ were limited to this life only we should, of all mankind, be the most to be pitied" (1 Corinthians 15:17,19).

If Jesus did not conquer death, then he can be dismissed as one more innocent victim, possessed of good but impotent intentions, who was abandoned by his friends, his nation, and his God. If Jesus did not rise, then his last words, uttered in agony from the cross, would end his story: "My God, my God, why did you forsake me?" (Mark 15:34); "It is finished" (John 19:30).

Paul himself, who could not claim to have known Jesus in the flesh, nevertheless counted himself as one of the many witnesses of the *risen* Christ:

He was seen by Cephas, then by the twelve, and subsequently he was seen simultaneously by over five hundred Christians, of whom the majority are still alive, though some have since died. He was then seen by James, then by all the messengers. And last, as if to one born abnormally late, he appeared to me! (1 Corinthians 15:5–8)

Unlike the gospel accounts, in which Jesus' death and resurrection were presented as stories calling for faith, Paul, when he penned this letter, in A.D. 55 or 56, presented the testimony of eyewitnesses who were alive at the time he became a Christian and an apostle. His account—far from being a pious memorial to the ideals of a dead man—is based on direct experience of the resurrected Christ, not just on faith. The doubting apostle, Thomas, had even more evidence, as the risen Lord invited him to "put your finger here—look, here are my hands. Take your hand and put it in my side. You must not doubt but believe" (John 20:27).

Subsequent skepticism about the resurrection stems largely from overanalysis. Eyewitnesses agreed only that Jesus truly died and that Jesus was newly alive—not simply restored to his previous life. He was the same, yet somehow different. Since no one witnessed the *process* of resurrection, the religious art that attempts to depict it is fanciful and invites mockery. Over the course of nearly two millennia essential facts have been buried in speculation. They merit our interest.

## A New Life

The resurrection of Jesus was not at all a miracle like the reviving of his friend Lazarus. Miracles are *exceptions;* but once Jesus rose, resurrection became the new rule for everyone. On account of Christ we can no longer escape eternity. During his ministry, Jesus miraculously raised people from the dead, but only to restore them to the same temporal lives from which death had snatched them prematurely. They would die again. By contrast, Jesus died but once, and his life was not simply resumed, but transformed, in his resurrection. That is the miracle in which we will participate. We will be transformed.

Dying on the cross, Jesus was taunted by his enemies: he saved others; could he not save himself? To be sure, before his arrest Jesus had prayed that he might be spared death; but he concluded his prayer with acceptance of God's will, which was that one man die that all might live—not longer lives, but transformed and eternal lives.

Throughout history, great monuments have been dedicated to dead heroes, and pilgrimages made to their graves. In the case of Jesus, there has never been an elaborate cult surrounding his tomb; we are not even sure where it is. No matter: it did not hold him long.

Contrast Christianity's lack of interest in Jesus' grave with its almost mystical veneration of his cross and the Holy Grail—the cup Jesus offered his apostles at the Last Supper, indicating: this is my blood. These few memorials, plus his words and his Spirit, are what Jesus left behind. The rest he took with him into glory. All that he cared for and all that he loved, he carried with him into eternity. So will we take with us everything we value.

## *Belief in a Resurrection*

The contrast between Christian and Jewish expectations of an afterlife is dramatic, and it explains why Christian apologists grasped at isolated passages in the Old Testament to find anticipations of what Jesus later accomplished. Unfortunately, contemporary biblical scholarship does not support conformity between the testaments in this regard. On analysis, passages from the prophets, seized by Christian apologists to prove that the earliest revelation included an expectation of resurrection, are less than literal. For example, when Hosea says, "After a day or two he shall bring us back to life, on the third day he will raise us and we shall live in his presence" (Hosea 6:2), the prophet is referring directly to the rehabilitation of the demoralized Israelites over a short time. Likewise, when Ezekiel presents his famous vision of dry bones coming to life, the context suggests that the prophet is only referring to a new life in Israel for the Jews returning from exile, their Babylonian captivity.

In time, however, the Jewish experience of exile and persecution put pressure on the accepted notion: that all accounts are settled in the present life. Unhappily, the Jews were called to obey their God in the face of blatant and unresolved conflict. Wicked nations and individuals trod on the innocent and faithful Chosen People, and too often triumphed. Accordingly, a new expectation began to grow: that justice and fulfillment must come in a future life.

We find an intimation of this in the book of Daniel, purporting to describe events in the sixth century B.C. but probably written four centuries later, in yet another time of persecution. The author speaks of a future time of great distress when "of those who lie sleeping in the dust of the earth, many will awake, some to everlasting life, some to shame and everlasting disgrace" (Daniel 12:2). The stress here as elsewhere is on the eventual restoration of Israel, but the new feature is that the dead will rise. In these late centuries of national oppression before the birth of Jesus, the question was increasingly asked: what is the point of being a martyr if there is no justice here or hereafter?

This question is answered dramatically in the Greek Old Testament, in the second book of Maccabees. The story concerns seven brothers and their mother who one after another undergo martyrdom rather than violate God's law. As the eldest brother is mutilated in the presence of the king, his family calls on God, invoking the Torah: "The Lord is watching . . . he will certainly take pity on his servants" (2 Maccabees 7:6; Deuteronomy 32:36).

As the second brother is executed, "with his last breath he exclaimed, 'Inhuman fiend, you may discharge us from this present life, but the King of the world will raise us up, since it is for his laws that we die, to live again forever'" (2 Maccabees 7:9). The third brother to be executed proclaims: "It was heaven that gave me these limbs; for the sake of his laws I disdain them; from him I hope to receive them again" (2 Maccabees 7:11). The brothers' mother nails home this new expectation—"It is the creator of the world . . . who in his mercy will most surely give you back both breath and life" (2 Maccabees 7:23)—and assures them that she will see them again.

The principal drama of Maccabees is that, challenged by enemies who have the power to destroy his creatures, God vindicates himself and delivers justice by restoring life. Thereby God reassures those who remain faithful to him in the midst of trials and gives them certain hope. Ultimately, no one can destroy us or take anything from us. Only we can rob ourselves of our inheritance by rejecting God.

## Our Great Expectations

In Jesus' time, despite a growing belief in an afterlife, many Jews lived in expectation that justice might after all be restored in the present life, not after death—that God's kingdom was imminent. This popular mentality explains much of the confusion surrounding Jesus. In his preaching, he nourished the messianic dream by proclaiming that the kingdom was at hand, thereby raising popular expectations while drawing political opposition from an establishment that resented his claim of authority. The crowds, yearning for justice after centuries of oppression, were mostly deaf to Jesus' explanation that his kingdom was not of this world.

Ironically, the earliest generations of Christians perpetuated this same enthusiasm for an imminent kingdom of glory with Jesus as its head. But neither the Jewish nor the Christian hope was satisfied in these terms. The temple in Jerusalem was destroyed in A.D. 70, never to be rebuilt. Jesus' apostles and generations of Christians went to their graves after proclaiming a kingdom that never came to pass.

Or did it? According to the Christian faith, God's kingdom was restored when Jesus took on the sins of the people, died, and was raised up by the Father. Eyewitnesses attested to seeing the risen Jesus—now Christ and Lord. What no one could verify with his eyes was that, because of Jesus, all creation was redeemed. That would require faith. Estranged from its Creator for countless centuries since Eden, mankind was now once and for all reconciled to God through Jesus' self-sacrifice. With his resurrection, he became Lord of a kingdom that embraces both this world and the next.

There is no new revelation contained in Easter except that Jesus is now Lord and Christ. But the events of Easter are the foundation of Christian belief. At the outset of his career Jesus said simply, "Follow me." The resurrection reveals where he is leading his creatures: to a transformed life that is eternal.

Before the events of Easter, Jesus and his adherents constituted only a deviant sect within Judaism. But Easter created Christianity—a New Covenant with God continuous with the old but now professing faith in Jesus of Nazareth as the living and reigning Christ. Christians henceforth no longer simply emulate Jesus the moralist and teacher; they follow Christ the Lord of life into eternity with the Father.

## *Our Transformation*

While the temptation to imagine the shape of eternal life is irre-
sistible, it is ultimately fruitless. Jesus' own resurrection reveals
no details of how the event was achieved—only *that* it happened.
The risen Christ appears suddenly, yet is elusive; he is tangible,
yet somehow immaterial. While conceding with Paul that "eye
has not seen nor ear heard" what God has in store for those who
love him, we can nevertheless confidently conclude that we will
rise as whole persons. Unfortunately, we persist in defining ourselves as creatures composed of a body and a soul, even as we concede that neither our physical nor psychical selves can function
separately.

In the last century, it was fashionable among skeptics to reduce
the soul to brain matter—gray jelly contained in one's cranium.
But that was patently inadequate as an explanation. The soul can
no more be conveniently reduced to one's nervous system than
one's body can be dismissed as a robotic contrivance driven by
one's soul. Our conscious life, emotions, personality, ideals, and
very identity require a brain, but cannot be reduced to gray matter. Watching a football game on television, I can agree in the ab-
stract that the picture depends on a consistent stream of electrons
bombarding a fluorescent screen, but that does not reduce football
to an electric current. Fortunately, we need not fully comprehend
our existence as human beings to understand that we cannot function without both our body and our soul working as a unit.

Being a typical middle-aged male, I think about my body only
when I am ill, or when confronting a mirror, or when shaving, or
buying a new suit. If challenged, I would define my self as my
thinking, feeling, worrying ego. Even when my stomach is empty,
I do not conclude that my *body* is famished, but only that *I* feel
hungry. Nevertheless, if we had the opportunity to meet, I would

be aware of you as *physical*. After all, I cannot read your thoughts and emotions; I only surmise that you have a psyche because I have one. (It's conceivable to me, an outsider, that you could be a robot!) This helps to explain why, when we encounter a corpse or even a sleeping person, we are discomfited: the conscious person we assume controls a body is no longer in command. All we see is the physical remains.

Despite the predilections of Plato, it is no more sensible to believe in the *pre*existence of souls than in their persistence after death. Practically speaking, the soul is an abstraction; it cannot function without the body it enlivens. It is pointless to survive on its own, for that would mean we would be less in eternity than we are here and now in time. Resurrection is not partial. Like Christ, we will be re-created as whole persons, fit not simply for a few more years marked by aging and declining powers, but for an eternity with God. Resurrection carries not a lifetime warranty but an eternal one.

Until very recently, the expectation of bodily resurrection motivated the Christian preference for burial rather than cremation and perpetuated the tradition of preserving the body for viewing before interment. Christians reasoned that the body, whatever its condition, was the temple of the Spirit and deserved respect. The current fashion for cremation rather than interment (and memorial services in place of funerals) is not without practical merit but tends to foster the notion that only the soul—or the memory of the deceased—survives.

## Becoming Whole Again

When the Christian creed proclaims faith in the *resurrection of the body,* it accepts the dichotomy of body and soul, but affirms our wholeness in the new creation. We can only wonder about our age and physical appearance in eternity, but appearances will not matter. We will retain our identity and our personal history. Beyond sustaining that sameness and gaining the company of God, we are reduced to speculation, and our imaginations are not up to the task. In the Catholic Mass for the dead, it is stated confidently that "life is changed, not ended." We will undergo a metamorphosis, shrugging off our limitations as we penetrate the infinite. In our resurrected state, we will altogether transcend the impersonal; everything will be personal. Not only will we meet God face-to-face, but we will meet one another as well—and indeed, truly confront ourselves. Although such a naked prospect of self-knowledge is frightening in this life (when we expend so much energy in avoidance and indirection), it can lead to remorse and redemption. Nevertheless, in eternity we can be confident that, with all barriers breached, we will achieve fulfillment and consummation. Experiencing fully God's love for us, we will at last be reconciled with ourselves.

It is important to identify the source of Christian confidence that we *can* and will take everything good from this life with us into the next. Strictly speaking, it is not faith in the resurrection, an event that is history. Rather, believers place their faith in the risen Christ, who is ever present and eternal. As Christ's cross was the key to his resurrection, it remains the effective symbol for the life of faith. It is a tribute to the soaring confidence of the first Christians that they made the cross—the sign of Jesus' apparent shame and failure—the permanent symbol for his triumph and ours.

In the course of the present life we die many small deaths before our definitive end and rebirth. Lamentably, we become life's enemies through betrayal and indifference, irresponsibility and disdain. To be a Christian is to affirm and nurture life and to see the cross not only as the symbol of victory but as the sign of the suffering that is the test of love that won eternity.

## *The Meaning of the Ascension*

On the face of it, Jesus' resurrection is complicated by his subsequent ascension into heaven, because it tempts us once again to visualize eternity as a place "up there" in which the risen Lord occupies space. Biblical scholarship suggests that the evangelist Luke, who was not a witness to the resurrection, introduced an account of an ascension into both his gospel and his Acts of the Apostles as a device to close out Christ's earthly career and to underline that in eternity he is the risen Lord and Messiah.

Luke is determined that Jesus' accomplishment not be restricted to a small band of followers eager for an imminent Second Coming, but that he be proclaimed to the ends of the earth and to all future generations. There must be a definitive, dramatic leave-taking, so that the church, enlivened by the Spirit, may set about its business to preach the risen Lord with confidence. If you are like me, you cannot altogether shake the mannered Renaissance depictions of Christ ascending into a bank of clouds; but all Luke means to express by clouds is the concurrent immanence and immateriality of God in this farewell scene. What could be more visible, yet less tangible, than a cloud!

Upon Christ's disappearance, the evangelist underscores his lesson: "Men of Galilee, why are you standing here looking up into the sky? This very Jesus who has been taken up from you into Heaven will come back in just the same way as you have seen him go" (Acts 1:11). Hans Küng explains that those who grasp the true meaning of Easter are not those who gaze up into the sky but those who bear witness to Jesus in the world.

## *The Seed Sown Will Bloom Again*

At the funeral of the legendary conductor Hans von Bülow, composer Gustav Mahler cried out to his dead friend: "Why have you lived? Why have you suffered? Is it all a huge, frightful joke?" As if in answer, the church choir intoned the words of Klopstock's ode "Resurrection":

> *I came from God and will return home to him . . .*
> *My dust will rise again . . .*
> *The God who calls me will grant immortal life;*
> *The seed he sowed in me will bloom again.*

The following year Mahler incorporated these lines in the finale of his Second Symphony, which he entitled *Resurrection,* and he appended these words:

> *Have faith, my heart: you have lost nothing.*

This is the promise of eternity, where all we have learned and loved and accomplished need no longer be recalled as mere memory but will be instantly relived in an eternal present. The promise of eternity makes it all the more imperative that we fill our present lives with *portable* goods—the permanent passions of the heart and mind that make life this side of death worth living. Leave behind the fashions and the habits you have outgrown. Nor will you need the nostrums from your medicine cabinet in eternity. You *can* take the best with you, in the firm faith that you were made for Paradise and that Paradise was created for you.

## *Traveling Lightly*

Frequent travelers learn to be discriminating about what they pack and carry on their journeys. The experienced business traveler carries a bag just large enough to tuck under an airline seat. The alternative is onerous—to lug and check heavy baggage and, on arrival at one's destination, to wait for it to appear on the airport carousel.

I have yet to encounter a traveler who regrets traveling light. Frequent travelers feel free because they know exactly what they need. The actor Clint Eastwood is a millionaire many times over, yet he travels with only a change of clothes, washing out shirts, socks, and underwear in hotel rooms. Perhaps he learned the value of traveling light from the many Westerns in which he starred. Only essentials can be carried in saddlebags.

When Jesus equated the difficulty of a rich man entering the kingdom of heaven with a camel passing though the eye of a needle, he was not condemning wealth but extolling the practical wisdom of traveling light. In our ultimate journey from life to eternity we cannot carry everything with us, but rich and poor alike can take everything of value.

When Abraham Lincoln married, he had his wife's wedding band engraved with the words "Love is eternal." As you prepare for eternity, you will separate the substantial from the merely ephemeral things in your life. Love is one of the things you will take along because eternity is ruled by affection, and love travels lightly. So does friendship, knowledge, gratitude, truth, beauty, humor, and appreciation. Living in the light of eternity means packing wisely now for our final destination.

# FOUR

# THIS TRIP IS NOT A VACATION

What no eye has seen, nor ear heard, nor the
heart of man conceived . . . God has prepared
for those who love him.

1 CORINTHIANS 2:9

Given the choice between going to heaven and hearing a
lecture about heaven, Oscar Wilde noted, an American
would take the lecture. The English wit's indictment is true
enough to be discomfiting. Talk is reassuring, a buffer
against reality. It explains why we chatter so long on the tele-
phone. By contrast, silence is unnerving, experience scary.
We prefer impersonal adventures on the wide screen rather
than in our lives. Virtual reality beats the real thing. We are
quick to heed the warning "Don't attempt this at home."

Moslems are required at least once in their lifetime to
make a pilgrimage to Mecca, presaging their ultimate journey to Paradise. It is an onerous journey, even for the
wealthy, contrived to make the faithful take thought about
the balance of their lives on earth. The afterlife will be our
ultimate adventure as well—a very foreign adventure unless
we prepare now. Is our passport in order? Will we speak the

language there and comprehend the customs of the inhabitants?

Our final trip will not be a holiday, but our eternal destination. Prayer is our passport, silence the language spoken there, love the custom of the natives in that place. Better that we prepare for the journey than be shanghaied into eternity.

ৡ

VACATIONS ARE TEMPORARY GETAWAYS for which we purchase round-trip tickets. By contrast, the trip to eternity is one-way and permanent; it is our journey home to stay.

Until recently, religion was routinely reviled for offering mortals an escape from life on earth. Today, ironically, men and women are tempted to escape *into* the distractions of everyday life to avoid contemplating the future. Not long ago, when life expectancy was brief and infant mortality was high, death was an unavoidably common experience. It happened at home. Today, fictional death is something that entertains us in the movies, while real death is something we only read about in the newspapers. Out of sight, out of mind.

Not only are we tempted to retreat from reality; we sanitize our daily experience, sequestering the sick behind hospital walls and shuffling off the aged to nursing homes. Many Americans now reach late middle age before death claims any person close to them. Then it is typically their parents, whose decline was not apparent because (unlike earlier generations), adult children now live apart from their parents. Living generations not only enjoy a longer life expectancy but are spared even the intimation of mortality until the winter of life sets in.

Legend has it that the Buddha's conversion from pampered prince to religious leader occurred when he first experienced poverty, sickness, and death among those less privileged than he. His way of dealing with mortality was to deny its hold and to seek serenity by emptying his senses. By contrast, Christians celebrate creation and regard its corruption only as a temporary loss of integrity caused by mankind's pride, later rectified through Jesus' sacrifice. Death neither attracts nor deters the Christian, who is not morbid but accepts life as a gift, while acknowledging its shortcomings this side of eternity.

For the Christian, eternity is not an escape from life but its fulfillment. Men and women are not second-rate spirits condemned to live in the prisons of their bodies, but were created to live in Paradise. This was how life for humankind was meant to be and as it will be again eternally in heaven.

## Heaven Is What You Bring to It

Generations of Sunday school teachers have persuaded their young charges that heaven will be the reward for a lifetime of good behavior. Those tots grow into adulthood trusting that, so long as they toe the line, they will escape perdition and live happily ever after in heaven. It is a paltry prescription for living in the light of eternity.

To give our teachers their due, they were appealing to our better natures, and they affirmed that God is eternally generous. What they failed to do was to focus our present lives on our common destiny. Inadvertently, they reduced religion to morality, and they persuaded us that heaven is a reward we purchase by good behavior. With every good intention, they depicted God as a demanding parent and separated our present lives from the life we will lead forever after. They created a moat in our minds and our hearts between earth and heaven. As adults, we must bridge that moat.

Living one's present life in the light of eternity is not unlike planning for retirement. Working people anticipate their golden years but don't pretend that they are a reward for good behavior. To retire comfortably and securely, one needs to invest wisely and set sensible priorities. Equally important, future retirees must develop interests in early adulthood that they can more fully enjoy in later years.

Without activity and passion as motivators, retirement can become a living hell. I know colleagues who have become so depressed in retirement that they can hardly bring themselves to dress and shave in the morning. Heretofore, their lives were wholly preoccupied by their careers. They never learned to enjoy themselves. Having neglected to cultivate their minds, bodies, and emotions, they now find retirement to be a curse rather than a reward. Some, who took their marriages for granted during their working years, now find themselves at home all day with their adult children departed and a stranger for a spouse.

To live each day in the light of eternity means opening ourselves emotionally and spiritually to our common destiny. It means developing the personal potential the Creator imbued in each of us—not just the ability to perform daily from nine to five and earn a paycheck. Contented senior citizens don't wait until they are drawing a pension before they learn to play golf or tennis, fish, travel, read, pursue a hobby, or volunteer their time for others in need. They don't put a hold on affection and intimacy in their lives until they have more time to express it.

Your heaven will be what you bring to it. As you sow you shall reap. The more you come to anticipate eternity, the more you will bring your daily life into conjunction with your destiny. Heaven, after all, is intimacy with God. Because God is love, love is for now, not later. God is truth, so it is time to fill our minds now. Because God is light, it is senseless to dwell in darkness. God is life and joy, so we must be fully alive now. Because God is our hope, we must be hopeful. God is compassion, so we cannot live within ourselves if we aspire to the company of heaven. God created both earth and heaven, the present and the hereafter. Life is God's blessing; we bless it in return as we prepare to live happily ever after.

## All This and Heaven Too

Compared to Christianity's lively depictions of Paradise and hell, its topography of heaven—our destination of preference—appears obscure and unimaginative. Of course, Hollywood's myth of a heaven consisting of clouds and angelic choirs is not only trivial; it is boring. One of Muhammad's great virtues was that he conveyed a compelling picture of heaven as everything you ever wanted on earth, and more. Although the Islamic notion of a sensuous afterlife offends puritan piety, it proved to be a magnet for the ragged nomads of Arabia, for whom life was, literally, a desert.

If, as its critics contend, the siren song of religion is wish fulfillment, one would expect believers to have a clearer notion of which wishes they expect faith to fulfill. In fact, most people have only the vaguest intimations of what might prove ultimately satisfying to them. Harold Kushner devoted a book to the issue, entitled *When All You've Ever Wanted Isn't Enough.* Rabbi Kushner's point is not that people are insatiable but that our pursuit of happiness lacks a reliable compass. We want to be happy but are aware of few things that satisfy us for long.

In a recent poll, the vast majority of Americans conceded that as far as they could tell, the rich are no happier than they are—supporting Saint Teresa of Avila's claim that more tears are shed over *answered* prayers than over those still awaiting a response. It is no wonder that heaven is elusive, when desire and satisfaction are themselves mysteries. In our constitutionally guaranteed pursuit of happiness, we Americans encounter the same irony. We are world experts on the subject of what makes us miserable, but hapless amateurs in discerning what will make and keep us happy. This uncertainty accounts, in part, for our erratic and desultory consumerism. We Americans shop until we drop, then hold a yard sale for the cast-off treasures that have failed to satisfy us.

Before I wrote *Spiritual Simplicity,* my attic and my life were clogged with things purchased for my pleasure that instead only gathered dust. A trampoline, weights, racquets, balls, skates, and fishing gear were reminders that I am neither sporting nor in sporting shape. My canoe still rests locked and lonely on a rack most of the year. A sauna in my basement might as well be an empty tomb for the use it gets. It is a fantasy in which I find insufficient time to indulge. The electronic equipment in my home and office demand devotion more than they deliver satisfaction. Despite my determination to unburden myself, the inventory of my errant investments in the good life remains long and laughable—revealing, in the end, that when left to my own devices, I cannot conceive of exactly what will make me happy.

## A Want of Imagination

Nevertheless, I have been surprised by joy, and others have shown me happinesses I could not conceive on my own, which suggests that fulfillment is not a do-it-yourself project. I never thought I fancied children until I had three of my own. Having put in their appearance after only minimal effort on my part, they proceeded to work their wizardry, transforming me into a more mature and less self-centered person—in short, a parent. I should have been able to predict my delight in producing three living dependencies, based on my own father's pleasure in me. If not quite heaven, my daughters have been a gift, mysterious and bewildering in content—in brief, a continuing adventure.

Nor did my upbringing prepare me for the keen, rich joys of

marriage. As an only child, I must have assumed my parents' purpose in life was to cater to me. But in regard to their personal relationship, I perceived them as friendly caretakers, or as an older brother and sister. What an awakening when, in my own adulthood, I discovered a woman who was prepared to be, simultaneously, my lover, friend, mentor, muse, teacher, nurse, hostess, chef, decorator, entertainer, and conscience—not to mention pianist, poet, novelist, composer, and educator in her own right! I sense now how the blind men felt after Jesus worked his miracles on them, for he did not simply *improve* their sight. Rather, as one exclaimed, "All I know is that before, I was blind, and now I can see!"

Accustomed as a child and young adult to dwelling in city apartments and suburban rentals, I was past the age of fifty before I conceived of living with a mortgage. To my utter surprise, a tiny town house indistinguishable from its neighbors became, by dint of monthly payments and devotion, not just a shelter for which I held the key but a nest and castle for my family. I went petless as a child because of my allergies to animals; as an adult, my weekly allergy injections allow me to enjoy cats and a Scottish terrier. The trade-off is more than worthwhile: my life, *in ways previously unpredicted and unpredictable,* is unimaginably richer.

When, during a dicey period in my life, I entered group therapy, I was struck by the scant perspective that people (including me) have on their troubles. Most unhappy people feel trapped for one reason alone: they are unaware of the options that might liberate them. They are their own jailers, pacing the prison cells of their lives, stewing in their own juices, cautiously hewing to the cowardly dictum "Better the devil you know . . ." Instead of exercising their constitutional right to pursue happiness, they rest on a treadmill that has stalled.

I risk belaboring this point because satisfaction, after all, is what eternity is all about. Some saints wore hair shirts and fasted. Others were imprisoned and fed to the lions. Monks and nuns to this day eschew married love and embrace regimens of prayer and asceticism. Even ordinary believers accept restraints and responsibilities alien to their impulses. Jesus himself endured agonies of anticipation in the garden of Gethsemane before his torture and execution.

Why embrace such rigors when the ultimate object of our common quest is joy? Is faith a form of masochism? Clearly, no one seeks a heaven of impoverishment and pain, but one of fulfillment. In this respect, the saint and the monk are more single-minded than you or I. Like athletes, they have their eyes on the prize and are determined to resist their reticence and strengthen their spirits to win. Athletes, both amateur and professional, train and often play in pain, dieting and denying themselves between combat—all just to win a *game*. Far from criticizing them for this bizarre discipline, we admire them and cheer them on. Indeed, we envy them their talent; if we had their ability, we would willingly embrace their asceticism. As for ourselves, the rigors of travel are small price to pay to ensure that we reach our final destination.

### Eyes on the Prize

A vacation is a diversion from everyday life, whereas our final journey is life's very purpose. We are inclined to fill our daily lives with distractions, some of them pleasant, but all of them invitations to aimlessness and dilettantism. You and I can wander through the department store of life as perennial window-shoppers and leave without ever buying a thing.

We would never think of going on vacation without luggage, but we must pack as well for our final trip. We will carry along all we have learned and everything we have cared for, every taste we have cultivated, every love and friendship, every kindness we have shown others. But there will be no room for cruelty, indifference, and irresponsibility in our baggage. We will leave care behind, but we will continue caring.

Only our Creator holds the key to our satisfaction, and the key is God himself. Faithful persons are not window-shoppers but buyers. They are not vagabonds but travelers with a purpose.

Relishing the prospect of heaven, William Booth, founder of the Salvation Army, predicted, "I shall have won the race. Gained the crown. Conquered the world—and myself." Mother Teresa of Calcutta, as tireless in our time as General Booth was in his, translated the efforts and sacrifices of her life of service as fulfillment in the next. "Heaven for me," she predicted, "will be the joy of being with Jesus—all of us going home to God."

Inasmuch as they are obsessed with God, saints are more interested in the personality of heaven than in its geography. For them, heaven holds out the prospect of being a honeymoon destination, and like earthly lovers, they are less concerned about their honeymoon destination than about their companion. If the personality of God is ultimately impenetrable to saints as well as the rest of us, there is nevertheless a rich history of speculation about heaven as a destination.

## Heaven as a Destination

Assuming the central tenet of Christianity is true—that Jesus rose from the dead and entered eternity in a glorified body, paving a path for all—then the heaven that is our intended destination is not just a love affair with our Creator but a place. And if there are other spiritual and purposeful creatures surrounding God (such as the angels), then heaven is a society. Something is going on there. Unlike vacation destinations, heaven has never put out a promotional brochure. But there is plenty of speculation about its features and the satisfactions it holds. There is a history to heaven.

Jesus' revelation is that God alone is sufficient for our fulfill-ment. Heaven is not about family reunions or lovers reunited—although that may be a part of its joy. The essence of heaven is a permanent love affair with our Creator.

We think of our final journey as a future event, but Jesus made it clear that the afterlife is present: "He is not God of the dead but of the living; for all live to him" (Luke 20:38). We live with God in the *now*. Jesus' promise of immediate entry into Paradise, di-rected to his crucified companion, he extends equally to everyone. But Jesus does not bother to explain how our bodies and souls are to be reunited after death. How we can have bodies in eternity is also of little concern to Saint Paul, who contemplated a transfor-mation more radical still that had already taken place. "I live no longer," he marveled; "but Christ lives in me" (Galatians 2:20). Paul suggested vaguely that we will exchange our physical bodies for "spiritual" ones.

Critics have attacked Jesus' vision of heaven as antisocial, when in reality it is radically pro-God: "No one knows the Father except the Son and anyone to whom the Son chooses to reveal him" (Matthew 11:27). For Jesus, to know God is the ultimate purpose of life. Heaven is our knowledge of God face-to-face. On returning to heaven, Jesus sent God's Spirit to dwell within each person and to *pray*—to connect us with the Father even before we make the fi-nal journey. Heaven consists of the perfect prayer: intimacy with our Creator. We have the Spirit to help us plan our trip. But Christian thinkers also had ideas about heaven and how to prepare for it.

## Heaven and How to Get There

The promise of new and eternal life was anticipated by the earliest Christians in the initiation rite of baptism, which persists. Total immersion in water signified not only a washing away of sin but, more important, one's death to transitory life and emergence into eternity. The newly baptized Christian donned white robes to affirm that he already had one foot in heaven and was beginning to live now in the light of eternity.

John's book of Revelation declared that (for humans, at any rate) heaven might be located on a renewed earth. During the first three centuries of the Christian era there was a widespread hope for a heaven on earth where persecuted Christians would be compensated for their privations. Against Gnosticism, which rejected the physical world as altogether evil, Irenaeus, bishop of Lyons (c. A.D. 140–200), championed a millenarian view that posited heaven as a restored Paradise. In his vision of eternity, the human body will be restored to life and placed in an ideal environment, enjoying renewed fertility, giving birth to new children. There will be neither aging nor death. Nature itself will be so fertile that no labor will be needed to find food. The Lord himself will prepare a table for the righteous, supplying them with all kinds of delicacies. In the heaven of Irenaeus there are no enemies. Even the beasts become tame.

That prosaic vision of heaven was in disfavor by the time Saint Augustine (354–430) made his appearance. With Christianity now the official faith of the empire, the age of persecutions was over, and asceticism replaced martyrdom as the surest ticket to our final destination. With his conversion to Christianity, Augustine exchanged a life of pleasure for one of self-imposed privation, motivated, in part, by a mystical experience. Augustine, then in his thirties, was convinced that he had touched divinity, if "just lightly," and concluded that "the greatest possible delights of our bodily senses, radiant as they might be with the brightest of corporeal light, could not be compared with that [eternal] life." He was "overwhelmed with joy and happiness."

This early experience forged Augustine's belief that heaven consisted of a direct and solitary confrontation with God, for which celibacy was an appropriate preparation. The dedicated Christian, he counseled, should be, "as far as I am concerned, a loner to the Alone." Aware that people would complain that a heaven without occupation would be an eternal bore, he countered, "Is this no activity: to stand, to see, to love, to praise [God]?"

In later life, Augustine's views on heaven became more social and less ascetical. He predicted that in eternity we would be graced with beautiful young bodies with which we would converse, eat, and drink. Beauty would substitute for sensuality. Noting the essential alienation of sin, Augustine surmised that in heaven human love would merge with the love of God. However, he predicted, there would be no exclusive intimacies in eternity, and no one would be a stranger to anyone else.

If Augustine's depiction of our journey's end strikes us today as austere, it may be because we lack the intimate sense of God that he carried with him ever since he touched divinity, "if lightly," as a young man. For Augustine, God was every satisfaction we know, every hope and dream, and infinitely more. Sixteen centuries later, it is Augustine's view that prevails more than any other in Christianity. He is heaven's travel writer.

Centuries later, Dante turned theology into drama. In the conclusion to his *Divine Comedy,* the poet, having passed through hell and purgatory, finds himself standing solitary before his Creator, absorbed in God's glory. Discerning the features of Christ in the light, the poet is overwhelmed by the love "that moves the sun and the stars"—surely more than anyone would expect from a mere vacation.

In his poetic vision Dante inquires of a saint:

> *"But tell me: all you souls so happy here,*
> *Do you yearn for a higher post in heaven,*
> *To see more, to become more loved by Him?"*

The response is negative: everyone in heaven, the saint claims, is content with God's will. They are all blissfully happy, consistent with the experience and affection they brought with them on their journey from life to eternity. The lesson is clear: we develop our capacity for contentment in this life. To live in the light of eternity means to expand our capacity now.

## What Is Our Pleasure?

Will there be only affection in heaven, or can we expect to indulge our passions as well? Scholastic celibates were ill equipped to address the medieval yearning for an eternity of physical and emotional satisfaction that the ordinary Christian could appreciate. The passion they address is unearthly. "The heart's life is love," declared Hugh of Saint Victor (1096–1141), having satisfied himself with the love of God. Revealingly, Saint Thomas Aquinas (1225–74) dismissed his life's work of theologizing as "mere straw" because he experienced on his deathbed a foretaste of the rapturous love of God. Passion appears to have its place in heaven for those who are prepared for intimacy. Unfortunately, many of us shrink from closeness in this life for fear of exposure. Living life in the light of eternity means nurturing our capacity for intimacy.

What is our pleasure? The answer we give to that question will define our eternities. It is conceivable that in some of heaven's mansions happiness consists of six-packs and sports on TV, but I doubt it. Heaven may resemble an extended sexual orgasm, but it's unlikely. Heaven is where love is, and love is not a solitary pleasure. In modern times people contract marriage for love. Songs celebrate love. Lovers sometimes take vacations to rekindle their passions. Although our final trip is not a vacation, can heaven be passionate?

During the Middle Ages, a secular tradition developed that

looked to eternity for a heaven of love between the sexes. Lancelot and Guinevere were passionate exceptions to the ideal of unconsummated chivalric love. It was not long before writers sought to reconcile human with divine love and, indeed, to claim that the love of a good woman could show a man the way to God. Dante credited his Beatrice for lighting his path to Paradise, and Petrarch longed to spend eternity with both Christ and his beloved Laura—"my Lord and my lady." Saint Bernard of Clairvaux (1090–1153) found the passionate songs of the troubadours a refreshing antidote to dry devotion. Only passionate, desiring love was worthy of God, Bernard affirmed.

Other saints argued for passion in heaven. Saint Gertrude (1256–c. 1302) addressed Jesus as her lover and spouse: "You are the delicate taste of intimate sweetness. O most delicate caresser, gentlest passion, most ardent lover, sweetest spouse, most pure pursuer." Lest contemporary Christians dismiss such love prayers as the fantasies of frustrated nuns, similar sentiments were being preached by priests of the time. "The King of Heaven," Stephen Langton (1150–1228) predicted, "embraces you with loving arms and bestows upon you the kiss of salvation."

For many medieval believers, the Blessed Virgin served as an antidote to what they had come to conceive as the awful austerity of God and the bleak prospects of heaven. Jesus' mother gave eternity a feminine touch. If motherly love did not quite rank with romantic love, it held the promise of affection and emotional satisfaction at the end of our final journey.

## Picturing Heaven

Vacation brochures promote their destinations with lush photographs. During the Renaissance, artists presented the faithful with panoramic depictions of what they could expect to experience at their final destination. Whereas Augustine piously mused about the blessed in their naked beauty, a millennium later voluptuous saints were being painted in gigantic scale on canvases the size of soccer fields. Despite the conventional inclusion of the Deity, these heavenly renderings increasingly came to resemble the frolics of nudists.

In the sixteenth century the Reformation reined in this Catholic celebration and restored the tradition of God as the essential subject and object of heaven. The Catholic Counter-Reformation supported this notion. Later, Protestant Puritanism and Catholic Jansenism further narrowed the focus of the Christian afterlife, downplaying human passion. As Martin Luther (1483–1546) had said of heaven's satisfaction, "I think we will have enough to do with God."

The Protestant Reformers were more concerned with practice than speculation—with ensuring that we complete the trip successfully. Death was certain, they affirmed, but salvation is wholly in God's providence. It was imperative that Christians order their lives responsibly in this world. Luther revived the early Christian notion that the earth would be restored after the last judgment as a reemergent Paradise. His fellow Reformer John Calvin agreed, and added that eternity would probably include plants and animals. Luther even welcomed insects in the afterlife but predicted they would be delightful.

Nevertheless both Reformers agreed that the restored earth would not be the heaven that is our final destination. It would be for contemplative purposes, not for habitation. Those who completed the journey would be otherwise occupied—with God himself. On this subject, post-Reformation Catholicism agreed with Protestants. As Saint Teresa of Avila (1515–82) affirmed: "God alone suffices."

As Christianity enters its third millennium of faith, an overwhelming majority of Americans still concur with the Spanish saint and the Protestant Reformers, professing belief in a heaven in which people who have led loving lives will be eternally rewarded. Surprisingly, only a minority of Americans expect friends and loved ones to share eternity with them, and fewer than one in five believe they will be busy in heaven.

## The Business of Eternity

So what's to do in heaven? A solid majority of Americans, regardless of faith, predict that they will be fully occupied in heaven by God himself. Only one in twenty Americans suspects that prospect might be boring.

My friend the English Franciscan Michael Seed relates an anonymous story he feels captures the essence of heaven as mutual love, and of hell as frustrated self-indulgence:

> In my dream I visited heaven and hell.
>
> In two separate rooms a banquet was in progress. Each guest had just one long spoon to eat with. In the first hall they were trying to feed themselves, which was plainly impossible, for the long spoons hindered rather than helped, and they were angry, frustrated, miserable.
>
> "This is hell," St. Peter explained.
>
> In the other hall all the guests fed one another, and they were happy. Then, smiling, St. Peter turned to me and said, "This is heaven."

For a recent book, Father Seed asked prominent, thoughtful people around the world what their faith has taught them to expect when they reach their final destination. Experts and amateurs tended to agree. For example, Archbishop Desmond Tutu replied that heaven will be an adventure of discovery we will delight in sharing eternally.

Actor-comedian Dudley Moore suggests that heaven will consist of an intensity of living that we are unable to sustain in this life. The Dalai Lama finds heaven in compassion and spontaneity. Former U.S. senator J. William Fulbright anticipates our destination as a "place of peace, a collection of inquiring minds, a community of compatible souls." In the view of the late C. S. Lewis, eternity will be "Chapter One of the Great Story which no one on earth has read, which goes on forever, in which each chapter is better than the one before."

Sir Edmund Sternberg, chairman of the International Council of Christians and Jews, favors a heaven that provides "emotional space to develop [our] hearts and attitudes, and physical space to train and relax [our] muscles." He visualizes heaven as a slightly distorted mirror that enables us to laugh at ourselves. (Saint Thomas Aquinas and Saint Augustine, incidentally, agreed that there is hilarity in heaven.)

Among artists, diva Joan Sutherland envisions heaven as "a reward—a peace of mind for faithful stewardship." Fellow musician Sir Yehudi Menuhin expects that heaven will increase his "capacity for wonder, ecstasy, and discovery." Novelist Morris West expects to hear the whisper "Be still. You are at home and safe!" Sir Peter Ustinov insists that "youth is not a time of life—it is a state of mind," and characterizes heaven as perpetual youth.

Novelist Graham Greene's sinner-priest in *The Power and the Glory* died with a smile on his face, signaling to his executioners his arrival in a better place. Our arrival in our final destination is dramatically described by the Vatican's chief dogmatist, Cardinal Joseph Ratzinger:

> In that moment, the whole creation will become song. It
> will be a single act in which, forgetful of self, the individual

will break through the limits of being into the whole, and
the whole takes up its dwelling in the individual. It will be
joy in which all questioning is resolved and satisfied.

No one expects a vacation to be more than a brief respite from
life's preoccupations. My wife reminds me that no one on his
deathbed ever expressed regret that he didn't spend more time at
the office; but at life's end, many people will regret that they neglected to devote sufficient time to affection. On reaching our final destination, we will be fully occupied with God, and love will
be heaven's rule. We would be wise to begin following that rule
while we still have time. Heaven is not a vacation getaway from
everyday life; it is our home. If we make love the rule of our lives
on earth, we are sure to feel at home in heaven.

# FIVE

# YOU ARE NOT GOING SOMEWHERE, BUT TO SOMEONE

"Is it easy to love God?" asks an old author.
"It is easy," he replies, "to those who do it."

C. S. LEWIS

Most hopeful mortals are still haunted by the twin enigmas of death and eternity. Each is a mystery, and it is only natural for us to shrink in the face of the unknown. But we can know more about mortality and immortality than many of us imagine—easily enough to enable us to live confidently in the prospect of eternal life, free of the fear of death. If you are a person of faith, this knowledge can give you both hope and direction. If you are a skeptic, you will be struck nevertheless by the convergence of belief, across time and cultures, affirming immortality. Either way, you will be able to approach your life with greater assurance and self-worth.

Each of us, by dint of our humanity, holds the key to immortality. Indeed, we cannot avoid eternity. Happily, the keys to the kingdom of heaven are sensible approaches to life that free our minds and spirits, not dogmas that shackle our souls.

**The beginning of wisdom is to view life and death as complementary rather than adversarial. Each of us lives and dies essentially alone. No matter how many friends and lovers we have, or how caring our families are, we are ultimately isolated in our own thoughts and emotions. Our separate bodies do not allow us to share either pain or ecstasy. Metaphorically, we are separate islands in life. But in eternity we will no longer be alone.**

ℬ

CHILDREN RESPOND DIFFERENTLY than adults to the question "Where are you going?" Adults will answer: "To the city on business." "To my office to work." "To the mall to shop." "To the beach on vacation." Children are likelier to respond: "To my friend's." "To Grandma's." "To my baby-sitter." "To my piano teacher."

On occasion, adults with children also admit they are going *crazy,* but my point is that children tend to identify destinations with persons rather than places. When Jesus said we must enter eternity as little children, this may have been what he had in mind. Because our adult notion of travel consists of maps and schedules, we are inclined to conceive of the afterlife as a *place.* Unfortunately, that forces us to attempt depicting our destination in terms of a travel poster featuring clouds and angels—and straining our own credulity in the process.

No wonder polls reveal that more Americans believe in God than in heaven. The numbers should be identical, of course, because *God* is what heaven is all about. Heaven could not be more personal; there is nothing else to it than the presence of God. "He's got the whole world in his hand," the old spiritual proclaims, which also says something about God's presence in this life. How much more will he dominate eternity! When we reach our destination, we will not be so swallowed up by God that we lose our identities; rather, we will be "absorbed" in him as lovers are in each other.

You will recall that when Einstein was asked facetiously what is beyond infinity, he replied seriously, "The face of God." In his allegory *The Great Divorce,* C. S. Lewis depicts an eternity in which we keep growing to gigantic proportions at the same time as hell keeps shrinking to the nothingness it deserves. Lewis's point is that evil—the denial of God or indifference to him—is emptiness, a vacuum, whereas God is everything.

In my everyday work in Washington, I often introduced speakers to audiences. Nowadays hosts introduce me when I lecture or appear on radio and television talk shows. Typically, I was not personally acquainted with the celebrities I introduced, but I learned what I could about them beforehand so that my lack of familiarity didn't show and cause embarrassment. More than once, however, when someone has been poised to introduce me, he has leaned over and asked, "By the way, who *are* you?"

We cannot enter eternity in ignorance of who God is. Having been formed in his likeness and having lived a lifetime as his creatures, we presume at our peril to knock on the door of eternity and blithely inquire who lives there. In all candor, we cannot plead that in life we never got around to God, as though he were a hobby we found neither the time nor the inclination to take up. The English novelist Anthony Burgess, who confesses that his faith runs hot and cold, also admits that he fears hell even more than he believes in heaven. Why would he be damned? "Oh, just human insufficiency," he allows. "Lack of charity. Self-indulgence. The usual faults. Failure of belief." He concludes, "There's certainly a hell. Everything we've experienced on earth seems to point to the permanence of pain."

But we are not condemned to insufficiency, lack of charity, self-indulgence, and faithlessness. They are acquired traits. One need not be "religious" at all to make God's acquaintance. He has revealed himself continuously over many millennia. Which raises the inevitable question: if we don't bother about him, why should he take us in? More to the point, why would we even desire to enter an eternity that consists wholly of God's presence if we offer him no place in our present lives? Hell is the sole alternative to God—it is his eternal absence. Whereas heaven is the obvious home for a concerned and loving life, hell is eternal indifference. We choose heaven or hell by what we value and how we live. The creator does not reject his creatures; but we are capable of rejecting God.

## Who Is God?

Were God subject to popularity polls, surveys would reveal an overwhelming preference for a user-friendly Deity who indulges his creatures from time to time but mostly stays out of their way. Ancient peoples were inclined to invent limited gods who possessed the facility of a plumber: someone who fixes something humans have broken (but can't easily repair themselves), and then goes away and leaves us alone until the next time we require his services. A convenient god would be one we could claim is always on our side of an argument: a bodyguard who could be relied on to intimidate our tormentors.

If religion were nothing more than wish fulfillment, then we might get away with made-to-measure designer deities. That is precisely what the ancients did, with great sophistication. But the God of Abraham, Isaac, and Jacob, as well as of Jesus and Muhammad, is nothing of the sort. He is intrusive and demanding, loving and forgiving, intimate and persistent. Even when he ignores our pleas, he never leaves us alone; instead he creates and sustains us and insists that he alone can satisfy us by his eternal presence.

But what can God conceivably have in store for "those who love him and keep his word"? The reticence of mainstream religion to do more than simply affirm the existence of an afterlife may reflect a certain disenchantment. The sentimental notion of heaven rooted in the Renaissance and developed through the Enlightenment and Romanticism does not square with the realities of the twentieth century—a century of total war and personal barbarity.

The heaven of entwined limbs and eternal hearths presumed that people were innocent at heart and could all be satisfied by the same things. A century of holocausts and unspeakable violence has shattered both assumptions. We do not know what will ultimately satisfy the human animal, but we have ample evidence that he will go to any length, including mutilation and annihilation of his fellowman, to pursue his unspeakable perversities.

We have learned to our regret that the human heart is not pure and humankind's intentions are not innocent. As we lurch into the twenty-first century with sufficient technology to construct a Paradise on earth, recent history forces us to ponder once again the demise of the original Eden. One does not have to be religious to wonder whether there is a flaw in human nature, a ghost in the machine, a virus in the programming that accounts for our perversity. And is that flaw inherited?

## The Persistence of Perversity

On the whole, Western civilization has been content with the notion that man is the measure of all things. Despite human diversity, it is argued, people all want the same things. If we are fed, clothed, educated, employed, and loved, we will be content, good natured, and a help rather than a burden to our neighbors. Modern societies have done all they can toward this end, with the exception of loving us. When, in the face of this faith, things go wrong and the human animal erupts in violence to himself and others, secular humanism rationalizes that his good intentions have been frustrated by some internal or external constraint. Free of oppression, the argument goes, we would all be content, loving, and neighborly.

Unfortunately, that secular humanistic faith has failed, but we are reluctant to acknowledge its collapse because we shrink from its alternative. The last time anyone took original sin seriously was in Puritan New England, but we want no part of reviving a repressive society.

There is another reason for religion's reluctance to declare much about the afterlife beyond hope for it. That reason is *caution.* The church finds itself sufficiently engaged in protecting revelation and affirming the existence of a spiritual dimension against the skeptical disinclination to look beyond this life. Being practical as well as serious, the church favors apologetics to speculation, scripture to fantasy. Above all, preachers do not care to invite mockery about matters about which they are themselves unclear, when they are already taxed to preach sound doctrine in season and out about things they do know. So, when enthusiasts claim out-of-body experiences, conversations with angels, and miraculous revelations, the church by its silence politely responds, "No comment."

Granting the practical wisdom of silence, religion's current reluctance to confront eternity unfortunately risks complacency about confronting God himself. If we dismiss the mythical depictions of heaven and hell of the past five hundred years, we must give some other substance to our hope. We are driven back to the original notion, backed by scripture, that eternity is the immediate and pervasive presence of God—that we were made by God to love and serve him and to find our ultimate satisfaction in him. Over the centuries, believers have confected a sentimental heaven that in the last analysis is an elaborate exercise in avoidance: a pleasant resort with such a busy program of pleasures that one need never meet the proprietor. By contrast, the accepted view is that heaven is not God's contrivance for our perpetual entertainment; heaven *is* God himself.

## *The End of Optimism*

Because they conceive of a purgatory where the soul can be prepared for God's embrace, Catholics find this traditional view of heaven appealing. Lacking this advantage, some modern Protestant theologians have felt constrained to conceive of moral development taking place in heaven itself—an evolution of character through enlightenment and service after death. Protestant theologians of the late nineteenth and early twentieth centuries appropriated from Darwin the notion of evolution, applying it to man's spirit, arguing that the Christian must work for salvation on earth and continue working toward perfection in heaven.

Preoccupied with attempting to build the kingdom of God on earth, practical Christians have been diverted from addressing the larger issues of faith, life's purpose, and the nature of God. Faith can be swallowed up in practice; devotion can be applied preeminently to work and only secondarily to God. This energetic, upbeat Christianity is the last hurrah for the old Puritan ethic, and it has persisted longer in the United States than anywhere else.

In 1933 the Scottish theologian John Baillie took exception to evolutionary optimism in his book *And the Life Everlasting,* sketching an alternative, neo-orthodox view of eternity. The First World War, economic depression, and the rise of fascism and commu-

nism exposed the prevailing notion of human perfectibility and
social progress as bogus. According to Baillie, a strenuous life of
service offered no assurance that the Christian was in an eternal
evolution of self-improvement. Baillie reaffirmed the centrality
of Christ as man's hope in this life and in eternity. But he could
not refrain from predicting some activity in heaven. "There
will . . . be plenty of room for adventure, and even for social service, in the heavenly life," he surmised, "though it will be adventure and service of a different kind. Instead of development *toward*
fruition, there will be development *in* fruition." After death, one
will see God and be transformed by the experience.

## A Cautious Christianity

"Ah! where the image with such warmth was rife, / A shade alone
is left," the poet Schiller observed, lamenting the loss of the gods
of antiquity. Schiller's sadness is echoed by contemporary Christians who, having second thoughts about the sensuous, sentimental, and strenuous heaven of the Victorians, search in vain for
something attractive to take its place. In 1979, the Vatican's Con-
gregation for the Doctrine of the Faith cautioned: "When dealing
with the human situation after death, one must especially beware
of arbitrary imaginative representations: excess of this kind is a
major cause of the difficulties that the Christian faith often encounters."

Contemporary Catholic caution is more than matched by the
Protestant churches, reflecting the difficulty of defending religious faith against the skepticism that has dominated Western thinking since René Descartes (1596–1650). That French
philosopher conceded "that by natural reason alone we can make
favorable conjectures and indulge in fine hopes, but we cannot
have any certainty" about an afterlife. Instead of speculation on

one's future, Descartes favored "clear and distinct ideas" whose truth was obvious to any reasonable person. Although he expressed personal faith in a life after death, he could find no evidence as to its nature.

The German philosopher Immanuel Kant (1724–1804) agreed that the world of the spirit lacks confirmation "because for this purpose no data can be found in the whole of our sensations." One must trust instead to reason, which lamentably "was not given strong enough wings to part clouds so high above us—clouds which withhold from our eyes the secrets of the other world."

Kant's skepticism about eternity influenced the father of Protestant liberalism, Friedrich Schleiermacher (1768–1834), who said of heaven that "we cannot really make a picture of it" because "our sensuous imagination is unequal" to the task. In *The Christian Faith,* Schleiermacher concluded that Jesus' statements about the afterlife were "all figurative, and not to be interpreted strictly," and claimed that Jesus "nowhere claims personal survival." His pessimism has been echoed by many thoughtful theologians since.

### Creating Heaven on Earth

If the pessimists are correct and eternity is "now" instead of "later," some Christians are bound to attempt to build the kingdom of heaven on earth. The American Walter Rauschenbusch (1861–1918) proposed that the purpose of good behavior is not to merit heaven but to improve society. In his *Christianity and Social Crisis* (1907), Rauschenbusch advised turning from the individual pursuit of perfection to the improvement of the world, hastening the "great day of the Lord for which the ages waited." In 1912 he wrote: "The Christian Church in the past has taught us to do our work with our eyes fixed on another world and a life to come, but the business before us is concerned with refashioning this present world, making this earth clean and sweet and habitable."

Rauschenbusch's new priority proved to be persuasive to generations of young Protestants. By 1961 fewer than one-third of American students in Protestant divinity schools expressed belief in "a real heaven and hell" and only one in fifty considered immortality to be a "major tenet" of the Christian faith. Yet fully half of the seminarians at the time hailed the Social Gospel as the Church's most outstanding achievement to date in the twentieth century.

It is noteworthy that the Social Gospel redirected the attention of Christians not only from the afterlife to the present life, but also away from the love of God as the primary purpose of life and the essence of eternity. Considering the state of the world at the millennium, the Social Gospel has failed, perhaps because of a flaw in human nature that perversely resists building a viable heaven on earth that everyone can enjoy.

Despite the hesitations of their ministers, American lay men and women maintain a widespread faith in individual immortality. They are supported by two theologians, the German Catholic Karl Rahner and the Swiss Calvinist Karl Barth. Rahner (1904–84) reaffirms that life concludes in confrontation with God: "The absolute deity will precipitate in unveiled nakedness into our narrow creatureliness." We can anticipate "an immense silent emptiness . . . filled with that mystery which we call God . . . filled with his pure light which takes away but also restores everything. Although the divine mystery remains undifferentiated, there also appears the face of Jesus . . . looking at us." However, Rahner dismisses altogether the sentimental heaven of a restored Paradise. All that surely remains of heaven, he concluded, is God himself.

## *Seeing from God's Point of View*

For Karl Barth (1886–1968) eternal life is "our manifestation with Him, with Jesus Christ who was raised from the dead, in the glory of not only the judgment but also the grace of God." We will see from God's point of view and understand how "our tears, death, sorrow, crying and pain" are linked to the "decree of God fulfilled in Jesus Christ." At death, the "veil will be removed, and our whole life, from the crib to the grave, will be seen in the light and in its unity with the life of Christ, in the splendor of Christ's mercy, of his grace and of his power."

Only a devout personal love of God can enrich the austerity of these theological visions of eternity. Ironically, contemporary secular culture has revived something like the traditional view of heaven. Modern Americans are better prepared to find the face of God beyond space because they are more conversant with space, having ventured there vicariously and often with their astronauts. From their home computers they routinely communicate in cyberspace. Moreover, as the literature of science fiction has gained respectability, it has made people more comfortable with the silence and void of space, and has stretched our imaginations with tales of time warps and telepathy. In science fiction, bodies are blithely dissolved, transformed, and reassembled, while the spirit endures. Contemporary people harbor hopes of transformation unprecedented in history, not because of religion but because of science and technology. Eternity is only one of them.

The genre of science fiction imagines new worlds and existences that bear scant resemblance to the heavens depicted on Renaissance church walls and ceilings. Its practitioners express little interest in the traditional heaven, but their fantasies contradict the rationalists who for centuries have discredited the ability of men and women to conceive of anything beyond the evidence of their bodily senses. Clearly our imaginations have taken up the task. The fantastic worlds of J. R. R. Tolkien and C. S. Lewis, for example, possess a charm and an integrity missing from our mundane lives. By design, a fantastic world is truer than our own. It provides a truer home than this unpredictable and contradictory vale of tears—exactly the advantage it shares with eternity.

But is heaven, then, only a figment of our vivid imaginations? To believe so would require us to welcome oblivion as our common fate, shrink our zest for life to these few precious years, render our aspirations for fulfillment false, and dismiss our hopes as fiction.

No, what our new fantasies reveal is that our imaginations are finally catching up with our convictions. God is no fantasy. We are real because he is real. On our ultimate journey we will not go somewhere, but to someone. If we live today in the light of eternity, God will not be a stranger when we arrive.

# SIX

# YOU ARE NOT READY, BUT IT DOESN'T MATTER

The point about Eden was that a man could live there as a man longs to live, but only as long as he longed to live as God willed him to live.

SAINT AUGUSTINE

Reverence is the foundation of faith, but gratitude is faith's motive. Upon waking each day, very young Jewish children pray gratefully:

Blessed are you, O Lord our God, King of the Universe, who removes sleep from my eyes and slumber from my eyelids. I thank you . . . for restoring my soul to me with compassion; great is your faithfulness.

We neither deserve eternal life nor can win it by our efforts. If heaven were only for the righteous, it would be woefully underpopulated. Jesus himself affirmed that only God is good; the rest of us struggle to be faithful, grateful, and repentant. We are never really ready for heaven, but it doesn't matter. It is God's gift to the grateful.

When you think about it, the afterlife is no more miraculous than the life we possess now. If the Creator chose to conceive the universe with all its wonders and bring you and me into existence, what would prompt him to discard what he values? His disappointment in us? Our failure to follow his blueprint?

If there is something in ourselves to be forgiven, he is ready to do so. And if, at life's end, we are still not yet ready for eternity with him, he will prepare us to be.

ฌ

THE EXISTENCE OF A PURGATORY is problematical. It is not at all obvious from revelation but is, rather, a logical assumption of the ancient church that fills a large gap in what theologians like to call the economy of salvation.

Purgatory answers the question: how do people enter eternity who are unprepared for it? To the good thief, crucified with him on Calvary, Jesus promised, "This very day you will be with me in Paradise." Because of his faith and change of heart, the erstwhile criminal was ready for heaven. But many mortals aren't. Their faith is fragile, their lives aimless, their morals erratic.

No one deserves heaven; it is a gift. But we must be prepared to receive presents. A small child is not ready for a Porsche; an obese woman is not prepared for Paris couture; a diabetic cannot appreciate (or even tolerate) a gourmet meal. If heaven consists, as expected, of eternal intimacy with God, some of us are ill prepared for the honeymoon because we have not lived our lives in the light of eternity.

No matter. If we are not ready, it doesn't matter. Heaven is like an open university, where we are accepted and enrolled toward graduation even if we have to take some remedial classes. Seeking to resolve the dilemma of inadequate preparation for our final journey, the ancient church posited purgatory—a state beyond death that provides a second chance to prepare to embrace eternity with our Creator.

Admittedly, nowhere is purgatory mentioned in the Bible. For all we know, God has other means of ensuring quality control and readying us for joy. But real or not, the concept of preparation is true to our experience of human halfheartedness. C. S. Lewis assures us that if a purgatory does indeed exist, the unprepared are in no sense condemned to it, but will choose it freely. There is, after all, no shame in admitting that one is not quite ready for God. A bride is not ready for her wedding until she gathers her trousseau. A surgeon is not ready to operate until he has passed his internship and boards.

If you were brought up from childhood as a Christian, you probably absorbed the notion that heaven is an eternal *reward* for good behavior. That is misleading—a line laid on children by adults to keep them from acting like little savages. "Only God is good," Jesus insisted, which explains why he exposed the hypocrisy of righteous rule keepers while he made sinners his friends and offered them God's forgiveness.

Redemption is a *gift,* pure and simple. Even the best of us must be pardoned, and forgiveness is unearned. To pretend that our virtue earns us the eternal love of God is to denigrate God's gift of his Son, who became human and died that we might live. Christianity maintains that the single question to be answered about the conduct of one's life will be: where was your heart? Purgatory is a contrivance for the vast majority of people whose hearts were not always in the right place.

## The Off-Center Heart

Salvation depends on having one's heart in the right place. G. K. Chesterton speculated that an intelligent alien from another planet, on seeing his first man or woman, would conclude that every human being is *duplicate,* our left and right sides being mirror images of the opposite feature. And indeed my left ear, eye, arm, hand, leg, foot, and toes closely mirror my right. Even in the case of a single feature—nose or mouth—the left and right sides are remarkably matched. (Our alien visitor would presumably be unaware of the vanity of actors who insist on being photographed only on their good side.)

On the evidence of his senses, our visitor would conclude that were he to open us up for a look inside, he would find two hearts, or at the very least a perfectly proportioned heart in the middle of our torso. And of course, he would be wrong. You and I, along with all our species, possess but one heart, nonsymmetrical and off-center. That is the physical condition of all mankind; in terms of spirit, we often operate off-center and with only half a heart.

Just as overindulgent Europeans of the last century made pilgrimages to spas to purge their bodies of the effects of bad living, we may realize on the frontier of eternity that we are not yet fit for God but need to strengthen our hearts. Perhaps purgatory is God's equivalent of the Betty Ford Clinic.

### Ancient Journeys

The earliest written evidence of grappling with the human journey from death to eternity is found in Egyptian pyramid texts as early as 2375 B.C. The dead pharaoh travels by solar boat to the sun god on an unceasing journey across the sky, or he joins a star, or alternatively ascends a ladder. Later Egyptian texts describe monsters and fiery lakes among the perils of the rehabilitating journey.

In ancient Mesopotamia, the goddess Ishtar journeyed to visit the dead. Confronted by a series of gates, she was allowed to pass only after divesting herself of an article of clothing at each. When she finally arrived before Ereshkigal, the queen of the underworld, the goddess was naked. Scholars speculate that the myth signifies death as the stripping away of life's functions, but it resonates in the Christian notion of an afterlife journey in which pretense, hypocrisy, and halfheartedness are sloughed away and the soul arrives naked before its Creator, just as Adam and Eve were in Paradise before their fall.

To guide the dead in their journey, Egyptians of the Eleventh Dynasty painted maps on their coffins. From the time of the New Kingdom (c. 1567–1085 B.C.), tombs were equipped with copies of the Book of the Dead, containing spells and other remedies to facilitate the trip. Orphic communities in southern Italy and Crete provided directions in gold inscriptions in their tombs. Much later, medieval Christians were counseled by a book, *The Art of Dying,* and Tibetan Buddhists (like the Egyptians before them) were advised by a Book of the Dead. The Greeks and Romans were even more practical, enclosing money in tombs to pay for passage to whatever lay beyond. The Greeks even thought to provide honey cakes to distract Cerberus, a vicious dog thought to guard the gate to destiny.

Jewish notions of purgation after death predated the Christian era by at least a century. Late Old Testament Judaism tended to believe popularly, if not officially, that the dead would be judged on the basis of deeds in their lifetimes and that prayers of the living for the dead might rouse God's mercy toward them. Although a few early Christian writers counted purgatory among required beliefs, it was not until the medieval councils of Lyons and Florence and the Reformation-age Council of Trent that the doctrine became authoritative within the church. Even then, apart from affirming its existence and function, and the ability of the living to assist the dead to reach heaven, Christianity shied from speculating about what happens in purgatory.

## Speculation Among the Faiths

From Christian antiquity, certain days were set aside for intercession on behalf of groups of deceased persons assumed to be in purgatory. A day for general intercession was set for November 2 by Saint Odilo, abbot of Cluny in the eleventh century. Known as All Souls' Day, it has been observed seriously by Catholics worldwide for nearly a millennium (and anticipated mischievously by children of all ages on All Hallows Eve—our American Halloween). All Souls' Day follows directly after All Saints' Day, which honors those already with God.

Moslems believe that, at life's end, they will be interrogated by two angels, Munkar and Nakir, concerning their faithfulness in life. Islamic martyrs will proceed instantly to bliss, but all others must pass through a kind of purgation until a final judgment, when their good and evil deeds are weighed in the balance. More dramatically, Zoroastrianism, founded in sixth-century Iran, predicts that after death each soul will wait for three nights by its grave, then, on the fourth, proceed to a bridge across which it may pass to heaven if its good deeds outweigh the bad. If the reverse is true, the bridge will narrow and the soul will fall into a cold and dark abyss to await a final resurrection.

In Chinese Buddhism, there are ten hells collectively serving the same function as the Christian purgatory, but with this twist: they purify the soul not for eternity, but only for a successful reincarnation back into the mortal world.

Purgatory, I think, has been unfairly maligned as a purely Catholic contrivance; that was its source, to be sure, but the concept emerged before the Roman church had any real Christian competition. Although the existence of a purgatory still makes a good deal of sense, at the time of the Protestant Reformation it was rejected on four counts: indulgences, revelation, grace, and predestination.

Every Protestant Christian learns as a child that the Reformer Martin Luther balked at the scandalous selling of indulgences. Like an itinerant merchant peddling patent medicine in the Wild West, the sixteenth-century Dominican friar John Tetzel was marketing indulgences in Luther's Germany, with the proceeds going to build Saint Peter's Basilica for the pope in Rome. Indulgences were calls on grace to assist the dead lingering in purgatory to get to heaven. The church reasoned that, since Jesus had given it the "keys of the kingdom of heaven," it could unlock the gates sooner for those in purgatory, who were no longer able to help themselves.

## *Speculating in Salvation*

Moreover, the church reckoned that Jesus Christ and the saints had accumulated more merit in their holy lives than they really needed for salvation, producing, in effect, a storehouse of grace that was available for sharing with the less virtuous majority. Indulgences, a call on this wealth, were like frequent-flier miles that can be applied to loved ones already dead. Whatever you think of the theology behind indulgences, the scandal consisted of selling them. To be fair, the church styled the transaction as a donation and expected the living to pray or do good works to activate it for the deceased. But in practice, unscrupulous preachers downplayed this part and focused on fear and superstition. Accordingly, when the Reformers rejected indulgences, they jettisoned purgatory as well—out went the baby with the dirty bathwater.

Luther pitted scripture against the institutional church and its tradition. The scriptural basis for the existence of purgatory was always slight, and came at the end of the Old Testament in a book that Protestants labeled as apocryphal anyway: "Therefore [Judas Maccabee] made atonement for the dead, that they might be delivered from their sin" (2 Maccabees 12:46).

Purgatory also ran into trouble in the Reformation because it assumed quantities of grace residing in the church as in a checking account, to be drawn upon by good works. Protestantism gave grace back to God to dispense as he chose, freely, and assumed that God either saved or damned his creatures at death, with no second chances beyond the grave. By reason of the original Fall from grace, most reformers argued, humanity was corrupted and could not earn its own way to salvation, even with the church's assistance. Only God could help.

In Luther's earthy terms, grace was dispensed to sinners as snow covering a manure pile. But the ultimate reason why the notion of purgatory failed to sway the Reformers was that many believed providence predestined each man to either heaven or hell despite himself. They reasoned that God, being who he is, is eternally decisive. The clear implication of Luther's challenge was that neither church nor creature can bargain with God. But the Reformers' objections still leave room for a purgatory that, far from being a factory of merit or place of punishment, offers the opportunity for transformation.

Grace, like snow, may cover up man's corruption in this view—but it does not transform him. God does not force salvation upon sinners; rather salvation presumes cooperation by man in his total conversion, which does not restore innocence, but makes him fit for God's eternal company. Some kind of purgatory that allows man to make ready for eternity continues to be credible.

## Problems with Purgatory

As a child in parochial school, I was taught that one went to purgatory as one is sent to prison—for rehabilitation over time—and that the experience, while unpleasant, was infinitely preferable to hell (which was analogous to the death penalty or life imprisonment). One would eventually be released from purgatory after some physical punishment to enjoy heaven eternally. By far the vast majority of the faithful were assumed to be in purgatory, so I was taught I could expect plenty of company.

Save for the aspect of rehabilitation, my childish understanding does not stand up to scrutiny. Purgatory was identified as a place of temporary punishment due to less-than-deadly sin. But of course there is no *time* in eternity for a sentence to be served. As for purgatory's rehabilitation being *physical,* that can be possible only for souls that still possess bodies. Moreover, conceiving of purgatory as a *place* makes no sense for souls, which take up no room.

As a kind of halfway house to heaven, however, it makes sense that we "sentence" ourselves to purgatory by our less-than-wholehearted behavior in life. Moreover, we should be grateful that God, our judge, gives us this second chance.

Nowhere is such a prospect of a second chance better exemplified than in Dante. Although his *Inferno* attracts popular attention, it is in his second book, *Purgatorio,* that the poet himself became a player in the drama of redemption. Dante was but a sojourner in hell; in purgatory he depicts himself as a fellow pilgrim, joining the inhabitants in their strenuous progress toward spiritual rehabilitation. Whereas his hell furnished a series of immoral models to be rejected, Dante's purgatory presents a cast of penitents, all journeying to God by subduing their willfulness.

Dante's purgatory, while no vacation, is no hell. Indeed, as the author departs his mythical hell for purgatory, he identifies stars unseen since Adam's fall. After hell's darkness, there is the intimation of a spiritual dawn. In Dante's vision, purgatory is a steep mountain to be conquered, but with levels of achievement for rest before resuming the climb toward eternal bliss. Revealingly, Dante wrote the book while in exile, underscoring his inability to find a permanent home in this world.

At the outset of his journey, Dante chose as his mythical guide through eternity the pagan poet Virgil, associated with the splendors of Rome. But at length, Dante finds worldly glory wanting and substitutes his real-life muse, Beatrice, as his guide to the liberating love of God. Having struggled successfully to reach the summit of purgatory and the frontier of heaven, Dante discovers himself to be renewed like nature in spring—"pure and made apt for mounting to the stars."

### From Myth to Understanding

John Ruskin cautioned, "You cannot make a myth unless you have something to make it of. You cannot tell a secret which you do not know." Dante's vision of purgatory is mythical but rests on the faith that God neither abandons his creatures nor flatters them. God is not only the supreme being, but also the supreme realist. If, therefore, something is to happen to us in eternity, how do we reconcile it with what we already know about death?

All we know from experience is that, when a person dies, his body is useless and begins immediately to disintegrate. We have no experience of our souls, however defined, operating at all unconnected to a body. Experiments with sensory deprivation suggest that when the senses cease to reflect external reality, we draw on memory and imagination: we hallucinate. But even dreams and mirages require a functioning brain—something lost in death.

Whatever a soul is, Christians concede that it is not better off for being without its body—hence the expectation of a general resurrection at the end of time. But this begs the question: what of those souls who do their "time" in purgatory before time ends on earth—that is, before eternity becomes all there is? Do they get their bodies back somehow before the end—as Jesus did? As regards purgatory (and hell, for that matter), how can a soul suffer all by itself without senses and emotions and memories—the physical requirements for both pleasure and pain? For that matter, how can a soul now in heaven be completely fulfilled in the absence of its body? Not to put too fine a point on it: it can't.

### Lessons from Beasts

Canon Charles Martin, the late headmaster of Washington's Saint Alban's School, was celebrated for his provocative prayer "Lord, make me the person my dog believes me to be." If you are not a dog lover, then trust those of us who are that canine companions are faithful to a fault—enduring war, injury, family breakup, physical separation, and even starvation out of sheer devotion to fickle masters. I have no wish to be a dog myself, but I would like to return to my Scottish terrier at least some of the trust that she lavishes on me.

In short, I should like to be—relative to my Creator—what my dog is to me: faithful, devoted, trustworthy, wholehearted, and generally fair tempered (terriers are not sentimental). Of course, while dogs can be kind even to abusive masters, that is not the case here: God in fact is gracious to me; it is I who am uncivil to my neighbor and unloving toward my Creator. My dog is not made in my image (she is in fact much handsomer than I am, but I do not let on); but God assures me that I am made in his image. Why, then, do I lack the innocent virtue of my own pet? And what can I do about it?

In the distant past, when theologians had nothing better to do, they wondered whether Adam and Eve's sin might have brought down the rest of God's creatures in their fall. Perhaps, some scholars speculated, wild animals are vicious and prey on other species because original sin upset the balance of animal nature as well as human nature. (You will recall that Adam and Eve were charged with naming the beasts but wound up acting beastly themselves).

In a Peaceable Kingdom like the original Eden, perhaps the tiger would not bare his claws, the bee would make honey but never sting, and the hideous serpent would be seen once again (as in Paradise) as the most beautiful of God's creatures. Though I believe this scenario to be metaphor, it contains enough truth to be useful as we contemplate our own unfitness to be with God—the rationale for purgatory. Carnivores, in truth, prey on one another not because they are naturally vicious but because they are naturally hungry. Only people kill from hatred. Animals may occasionally need to be restrained, but people need to be rehabilitated.

Animals fascinate precisely because they are so natural. When I go to the zoo to see the giraffe, I am not bored because he acts like a giraffe: his predictability is a delight. I do not go to the zoo to look at my fellow spectators, who on holidays are the most numerous of God's creatures in the park, not to mention more mysterious because they are unpredictable.

Human perversity consists in vainly equating our unpredictability with our kinship to God. My Maker has given me moral freedom, but (unlike God, who is consistent) I keep everyone, including myself, guessing. What will I do next? Can you count on me? Will I remain faithful and hardworking, or will my eyes, mind, and heart wander? Can I be counted on (like my dog), or will I follow my fickle emotions?

## Man's Best Friend

While there is no question that men and women are more intelligent than their dogs, we are not nearly as faithful. A dog can be trained to be a blind man's eyes, guiding him through a sightless life. But dogs do not find us nearly as dependable. Lamentably, the human being is the only truly wild animal, broken free from instinct and the unquestioning morality of the herd. We alone are capable of mischief, to the extent of killing for pleasure. God has refused to tame us; we must tame ourselves while remaining free.

What, then, is the advantage of being made in God's image? It is to enjoy independence and dominion, and to confess that we use these gifts badly. How often do you hear a person excuse beastly behavior by insisting it was the product of good intentions—the right instincts? The excuse falls flat precisely because we are not creatures of instinct at all, and the passions we sentimentally identify as instinctive are untrustworthy. Perhaps purgatory ultimately describes the process whereby I will learn to emulate the virtues of my dog so I will be fit to live with my truest, best friend—God.

## A Gathering of Ghosts

All this speculation about purgatory may seem pointless, given the fact that it is not clearly established on the map of eternity. Yet the premise of purgatory is sound: most souls, cut loose by death from their bodies, are ill prepared to meet their Creator. The mystery remains: what happens to them? As I was writing this chapter in a borrowed home in rural England, I came upon a book owned by our young hostess's son—about ghosts—and it occurred to me that these spirits may offer a clue to our quest.

A belief in ghosts may be nothing more than superstition, but it is striking that 25 million Americans claim to have actually *seen* them: not angels, mind you, but ghosts. Winston Churchill is only the most prominent person among many who profess to have encountered the ghost of Abraham Lincoln in the White House.

Although I haven't had the experience myself, otherwise skeptical friends of mine are certain they have (one family of friends in Virginia are convinced they host an entire ghost family in their home, which is built over an old Civil War encampment). If we are to believe reports, ghosts are mischievous, occasionally malevolent—and seldom helpful. They do not appear to be content; indeed, restlessness is their defining characteristic.

My only encounter with ghosts is in literature, and the most memorable is repeated every year with Charles Dickens's morality tale *A Christmas Carol.* "I wear the chain I forged in life," Marley's ghost explains to his erstwhile business partner as he sets the stage for Scrooge's trial and redemption. "Bah! Humbug!" Scrooge replies, attempting to dismiss the ghost's invitation to review his life in the light of love and eternity after facing the facts about himself.

To his credit, Scrooge sees the light after his dark night of purgation, awakening appropriately on the day of Christ's birth to his own rebirth as a man fit to serve God and his fellow man with faithfulness and generosity. Perhaps better than philosophers and theologians, Dickens grasped the purpose of purgatory: you are not ready for the journey, but it doesn't matter. With God's help, you will find your way.

# SEVEN

# BE PREPARED
# FOR SURPRISES

Our souls have sight of that immortal sea
Which brought us hither.
. . . . . . . . . . . . . . . . . . .
Though nothing can bring back the hour
Of splendor in the grass, of glory in the
flower.

WILLIAM WORDSWORTH,
"INTIMATIONS OF
IMMORTALITY"

There are two ways to handle a problem. One is to confront it; the other, to ignore it. Even the preferred path
seldom really solves the problem but merely makes it man-
ageable. This spring, for example, we discovered moles tun-
neling around our house. By persistence we can neutralize
them, but it will be an uneasy truce. They will not go away. An
armistice is not a victory.

We tend to regard death as a problem, ignoring its inevitability so long as we retain our vitality, confronting our
mortality only at the eleventh hour. Admittedly, we cannot
deter death, but we can conduct our present lives consis-

tently with the benefits we expect in the next. We will reap what we sow.

Philosopher Geddes MacGregor surmises that

it may be that some people, after a lifetime of selfish unconcern and of talk of nothing but the stock market and football scores and sex and favorite restaurants and the latest fashion in drapes, have nothing in them capable of surviving death. Who dares say?

We must invest wisely in our present lives so that we will have something in us capable of surviving death—and confronting the surprises of heaven.

SAINT PAUL, on being raised to the third heaven, reported "things which eye saw not, and ear heard not, and which entered not into the heart of man, whatsoever things God prepared for them that love him" (1 Corinthians 2:9).

We will certainly expect more in the afterlife than just the eternal rest that was routinely evoked at the many wakes and funerals to which my parents dragged me in my childhood. Before the current fashion for cremation and memorial services, open caskets were common and it was courteous to comment to the bereaved on how *peaceful* their late husband or wife appeared in death—something that struck me as not all that upbeat. God knows, life can slow a person down, but peace alone is a paltry payoff for a lifetime of wear and tear. The believer looks to God not for escape from life but for joy in him. If a Christian corpse's face reflected its real prospects, it would wear a smile. What sorts of adventures does God have in store for us in eternity? We can only surmise, but one helpful clue is that we will no longer be bound by time. Timelessness suggests that we will no longer be subject to physical aging, the slackening of the mind, and dulling of our senses. Nothing will tire us, and we need not postpone anything.

Computer manufacturers are currently contriving artificial experiences for us that they call virtual reality. The idea is to fool the senses into believing that something interactive is really happening—an adventure, a love affair, a trip through space. Of course, these manufactured experiences, however vivid, are contrived hallucinations, but entrepreneurs are betting that they will provide an oasis and a vicarious kick for consumers bored with reality.

Along similar lines, C. S. Lewis suggested that in eternity our memories will be just as vivid as our immediate experience. That means that you could relive your wedding day or the birth of your first child with total recall as a total psychophysical event, not simply as a daydream. Since eternity is outside time, any distinction between past and present would become irrelevant. If this theory holds true, our experience of the afterlife will be conditioned by the history of our experience in the present life. To enjoy art in heaven, for example, it will matter that I first took the time to cultivate the muse here. It is just possible that heaven will not completely compensate for anything we have missed in life but only deepen and enhance the experiences we bring with us. All the more reason to cultivate the good in the present life; we have more to enjoy in eternity.

## Splendor in the Grass

William Wordsworth, the poet laureate, fancied that every mortal originates in God's womb but, once born into life on earth, tragically forgets the eternal source from which he sprang. According to his poetic reasoning, we all experienced the afterlife in our *pre*-life but have no recollection of it. Long before the England of Victoria and Wordsworth, Cicero had lamented, "Not to know what happened before you were born is to remain always a child." The Roman was probably only urging the study of history, but Wordsworth meant more: life, he insisted, is amnesia, and this earth an exile. No study of history could bring back the hour of splendor in the grass, because it was an eternal hour.

Across the Atlantic, the poet laureate's American contemporary Joseph Smith founded a new religion based on the identical notion, persuading his Latter-Day Saints that, because they had been conceived in eternity, they were destined to return to it. Buoyed by such hope, the Mormons thrive to this day, having grown into a worldwide faith.

Wordsworth himself had no intention of founding a church, but rather of stimulating imaginations and awakening the senses of his compatriots. In our own century, the scientist Albert Einstein would agree with the poet that imagination is more important than knowledge. The afterlife envisaged by philosophers and theologians can leave the heart cold, whereas poets argue that beauty in nature and art supply superior intimations of immortality. Art not only selects and deepens experience but transcends the trivial and mundane, confronting us with ourselves, our origins, and our destiny. Heaven, artists contend, should not be the captive of the cloister; eternity belongs equally to men and women of passion and imagination. By this reasoning, we should be prepared for surprises in heaven but will not be caught totally unaware if we devote our lives to truth, beauty, and goodness on this side of life's frontier. History, however, illustrates that human imagination over time has been anything but consistent in depicting our eternal prospects.

## The Renaissance Paradise

Before Christianity, the popular myths of pagan Greece and Rome portrayed polytheistic eternities that were the antithesis of Jesus' heaven. Ancient Elysium was short on piety and long on splendor; its gods were fickle and playful. Hard on the heels of the high Middle Ages, Renaissance artists revived classical pagan themes to depict an ostensibly Christian afterlife that would have dumbfounded Augustine and Aquinas. While the traditional heaven had consisted (in Augustine's expression) of the soul eternally "alone with the Alone," Giotto in his great painting *The Last Judgment* in Padua depicted heaven as a vast society. Another fourteenth-century fresco, in Florence, joins Mary with Jesus as the focus of heaven. Notably, some of the attending blessed appear to be more interested in one another than in the beatific vision.

Byzantium departed even more from the medieval God-centered heaven of the Western church. In the view of the Eastern church, God resided in one grand but austere part of heaven, while the blessed inhabited another, more user-friendly place. During the Renaissance, heaven was often depicted as a city, the New Jerusalem, surrounded by a reconstituted earthly Paradise. A church wall in the Abruzzi painted about 1420 depicts heaven as a castle surrounded by a garden where the blessed, dressed in new garments, dance in ecstasy.

Rather than rein in the artists, churchmen of the time were persuaded by them to revise their conception of eternity. Savonarola in his *Compendium of Revelations* (1495) imagined heaven to be above a high jeweled wall encircling the universe. Although the fiery Florentine preacher was a member of the same religious order as Aquinas before him, Savonarola conjured a heaven his master would not have conceived as Christian. For

Aquinas, heaven was intellectual; for Savonarola, it was a spectacle.

Newcomers to Savonarola's heaven would be dazzled by light but could discern fields and flowers, clear streams, gentle animals, and an abundance of fruit trees, which were home to a multitude of songbirds. There the blessed could mingle and move with the angels. Unlike the immovable hierarchies of the medieval heaven focused on God, the blessed in the Renaissance heaven were conceived as mobile, ascending to the throne and swooping to Paradise at will.

The Renaissance Paradise was actually deemed superior to the original Eden. Now redeemed by Christ, nature was assumed to possess advantages over the primitive Paradise of Adam and Eve, and featured cultural anachronisms—fountains, boats, tents, and other accessories familiar to a cultured Christian during the Renaissance. Hieronymus Bosch (c. 1450–1516) honored the pagan convention of Elysium in his art when he housed the blessed in tents. The Elysian fields were more attractive to Renaissance artists than the claustrophobic cities of Europe, so they transformed heaven into a garden. Giovanni di Paolo (1403–83) attempted to improve upon Dante's *Paradiso* by depicting naked saints hovering like bees over the flowers of the garden, bathing or sunning themselves like vacationers. Aware that the beatific vision is eternally available on demand, Paolo's frolicking saints seem to be in no hurry for the next showing.

### Love in Heaven

While painters were altering the medieval notion of heaven, making it social and sensuous, Renaissance literature was injecting the new element of romance. Pierre de Ronsard (1524–85), first in line of modern French poets, introduced human passion into eternity, presuming against conventional theology that we can take our love life with us after death. Whereas Jesus had described a heaven without marriage where the blessed live like angels, Ronsard promised his beloved:

> *Bound together, kissing, we will go*
> *And cross the muddy lake below.*
> *Passing through where raging Pluto reigns*
> *We will arrive on scented plains,*
> *On fields that were decreed by gods of yore*
> *To be the fortunate lovers' shore.*

It is tempting to dismiss Ronsard's paradise as a blatant restoration of the pagan heaven, but in Renaissance Europe there could be but one afterlife—and it was Christian. Rather than dismiss classical themes as pagan, Renaissance theologians in effect baptized them. Lorenzo Valla in his dialogue *On Pleasure* (1431) predicted that, after death, the blessed are welcomed to heaven by family, friends, and saints. The Mother of God, he predicted, "will clasp you to her virginal breast on which she suckled God, and she will kiss you." In heaven, our bodies will be captivated with a delight "that thrills you to the marrow, so that no venery can be compared to it." Valla's heaven promises sensuality without guilt. Aware of treading on dangerous ground, he advised that the principal delights of heaven will consist of intellectual pleasures such as the mastery of languages, arts, and learning. In 1440 Donatello expressed Valla's ideas in painting the gallery of the cathedral in Florence.

Fra Angelico's *Last Judgment* in Florence attempted a compromise by joining the conventional medieval heaven of contemplation with a sentimental paradise in which a celibate monk is shown embraced by a feminine angel. The blessed of Angelico's painting are not canonized saints; they are only ordinary Christians enjoying their rewards for faithful living on earth. Whereas martyrs had been preeminent in the traditional heaven, the new heaven jettisoned heroism and became democratized. Naive as these images appear to our eyes, they were accepted by sophisticated Christians of the time. When John Reuchlin died in 1522, the great Erasmus imagined his friend meeting angels and a special saint in eternity, all of them ascending to angelic music.

## A Material Heaven

The Renaissance view of heaven became progressively more sensuous and less spiritual. In the *Pleasing Explanation of the Sensuous Pleasures of Paradise* (1504), the glorified human body is described as young and beautiful, with sharpened senses and the ability to sing beautifully. It is assumed that the blessed will sing to God, but the saints will also have an enhanced sense of touch and will indulge it in mutual embraces. The book, dedicated to the pope, predicted that "the body of the lowest saint will taste fifty times better than honey." Its author, superior of the Canons Regular of the Lateran, hastily added that all these sensuous delights would satisfy the saints "without violating chastity."

Increasingly, the blessed in Renaissance depictions of eternity became more individualized, more beautiful and amorous, and more naked. At the height of the Renaissance, the Augustinian and scholastic perception of conflict between the love of God and the love of creatures all but disappeared. In the heaven of the Renaissance, the divine and the human were both satisfied. Despite having turned medieval conventions inside out, the Renaissance vision of the afterlife remained Catholic, rooted in faith and hope. With the dawning of the Age of Reason, however, that old faith would no longer be taken for granted.

Although Wordsworth had little in common with Emanuel

Swedenborg, the poet's yearning for "splendor in the grass" owes something to the Swedish scientist. Swedenborg dismissed the conventional heaven of faith on scientific grounds, claiming he had been there and had found it something quite different than others imagined. In his book *Heaven and Hell* (1758), the Swedish visionary substituted personal experience for the speculations of theologians and fantasies of artists, claiming that his heavenly visions occurred "while I was fully awake . . . and in a state of clear perception." Swedenborg eventually founded an alternative religion, but the Church of the New Jerusalem never caught on as an institution. Nevertheless, its founder remains significant to this day because his notions of the afterlife influenced all but the most reactionary artists and scholars until well into the twentieth century.

Swedenborg's heaven offered four distinct "advantages" over the traditional Christian concept of heaven: (1) it came immediately after death, with no intervening purgatory or wait until a last judgment; (2) it was not distinctly different from life on earth, but rather an extension and fulfillment of it; (3) it was active, not static; the saints kept busy becoming more saintly; and finally (4) God shared the focus of love in heaven with one's family and friends. Indeed, God in Swedenborg's afterlife is loved not just for himself, but through the love of the saints *for one another.*

Although the Swedish scientist is not much remembered today, during his own lifetime monumental sculptures in Christian cemeteries began to reflect his conviction that the deceased pass immediately to new life. Memorial statuary portrayed the dead as they appeared in life, often idealized as more handsome and youthful and vital than anyone's memory of them.

### Masters of Our Fates

Still others welcomed Swedenborg's conviction that the deceased remain masters of their fates in eternity, still able to change their minds and dispositions. By the Swedish scientist's reckoning, God is not the ultimate decision maker in heaven, and there is no final judgment. Moreover, leading an ascetical life no longer provides a surer entry into bliss. The rich enter heaven as easily as the poor, Swedenborg insisted. To ensure salvation, one need only be serious and responsible. Basically, the quest for paradise became a do-it-yourself project.

Whereas the Renaissance had portrayed a sensuous heaven but was reluctant to admit sensuality, Swedenborg insisted "from experience" that in heaven even the angels are sexually differentiated, enjoying all their senses. Indeed, he argued, angels were not a species apart, but only mortals like ourselves at a high level of spiritual development. Everyone in Swedenborg's heaven could aspire to be more spiritual, yet lose nothing valuable in the process. To his critics' observation that Swedenborg's heaven was too physical, the self-described visionary replied that spirituality is already preeminent in our present lives; our senses respond not to physical reality at all, but to spirit incarnate in matter. "Nature," he claimed, "was created simply to clothe the spiritual."

Some Protestants and Catholics welcomed Swedenborg's ideas and even anticipated some of them. For example, the German Lutheran pastor Philip Nicolai, in two books on heaven (1599 and 1606), parted from Luther by predicting that the earth would survive the end of time and feature flourishing cities and lovely landscapes. The climate would be temperate everywhere, and the seas would disappear altogether so no impassible boundaries might separate peoples. Distinctive languages would continue to be spoken, but as at the first Pentecost, everyone would understand them. What is most striking about Nicolai is his optimism about eternity and his upbeat reading of human nature. Goodness everywhere prevails, the future beckons, and the world will be renewed.

A generation later a fellow German, the Catholic Capuchin

friar Martin of Cochem (1634–1712), published religious best-sellers that were still widely reprinted into the twentieth century. In an appendix to his *Large Life of Christ,* Friar Martin located a material heaven on a restored earth. "What joys could the saints' five senses have if in heaven nothing could be seen except for a huge, immense space?" he demanded. So the friar filled heaven with "a real river, real trees, real fruit and real flowers that please our vision, taste, smell and touch in unsurpassable ways." Martin took literally the biblical expression that heaven consists of many mansions. Just as wall paintings had depicted Renaissance ideas about eternity, the ornate Baroque and Rococo churches of Friar Martin's time tended to reflect his enhanced, upbeat, and sensuous notion of the afterlife.

## *Work and Play*

In time, even the Calvinist tradition softened to accommodate the new heaven. Encouraged by Swedenborg, Reformed minister Johann Casper Levator published four volumes entitled *Prospects of Eternity* between 1768 and 1778, describing a renewed earth as mankind's eternal home. Striking a new note, Levator predicted that the saints would keep busy transforming the earth into Paradise. But eternity would not be all work and no play. "We will have bodies . . . deal with material sensual objects, and form one or more societies," he predicted. Eternity, he reasoned, would be a bore unless it included change, pleasure, and activity.

On the face of it, an amorous, busy, social heaven should have proved repugnant to conventional, God-centered Christianity. But that judgment fails to take into account the values the faith had to uphold during life on earth. After all, the church was on record sanctioning hard work, strong, loving families, and mutual responsibility for society's betterment. If heaven could be reconceptualized as the extension and fulfillment of these estimable earthly values, then perhaps people would be motivated to behave daily in a more Christian way. The old, arid, God-centered heaven was judged to be insufficiently enticing as an eternal prospect to encourage mankind's good behavior.

Wordsworth's high yearning to "bring back the hour of splendor in the grass" became popularized and sentimentalized, and by the time of Queen Victoria, heaven had been popularized as a kind of *Love Boat* cruise into eternity. Whereas Romanticism made heaven passionate, Victorianism would render it sentimental. Popular preaching and literature found respectable sources to justify this transformation. For example, John Milton's *Paradise Lost* had already recaptured the splendor of Eden before the Fall. Milton had mused:

> *What if Earth*
> *Be but the shadow of Heav'n, and things therein*
> *Each to other like, more than on Earth is thought?*

According to Milton, the biblical Paradise had been a heaven on earth. While careful to exclude vanity and lust from their lovemaking, Milton was graphic about Adam and Eve's "conjugal caresses." In his poem, Eve prepared the nuptial bed with flowers and perfumes; afterward Adam confessed to the angel Raphael that "here passion first I felt, consummation strange."

Later on, Adam asks the archangel Raphael how his fellow spirits manage to love in heaven:

> *. . . by looks only, or do they mix*
> *Irradiance, virtual or immediate touch?*

Raphael's reply is vague but not evasive:

*Let it suffice thee that thou know'st*
*Us happy, and without Love no happiness.*
*Whatever pure thou in the body enjoy'st*
*(And pure thou wert created) we enjoy*
*In eminence . . . Union of Pure with Pure Desiring; . . .*
*As Flesh to mix with Flesh, or Soul with Soul.*

## Priorities in Paradise

Milton acknowledged that Adam and Eve lost Paradise because they put their love for themselves before their love for God. But, he argued, their sin consisted only of getting their priorities wrong. The proper activity of Paradise (and heaven), he claimed, is love.

Human beings are unique among the creatures in their loving. Alone among the species, their desire knows no season. Alone among nature's females, woman enjoys sexual fulfillment. Moreover, unique among creatures, human couples across all cultures have intercourse facing each other. Contradicting all the humor expended on the missionary position, intercourse face-to-face makes love *personal,* which is why the Christian missionaries valued it.

The equality of the human sexes is reflected in the creation account where Eve is fashioned from Adam's rib. The moral of the myth is that man and woman, having been made *from* each other, are meant *for* each other. In creation, Eve is separated from Adam's body, which has prompted philosophers ever since to regard human love as the attempt of man and woman to rejoin "in one flesh." The romantic heaven would rejoin man and woman in a primordial unity of body and spirit.

William Blake (1757–1827) combined the talents of a poet and an artist. His advantage over most writers consisted in his

ability to illustrate his thoughts, which he did in a series of draw-
ings and watercolors depicting the afterlife. These he valued as
"stupendous visions." Only self-righteous and hypocritical people
are excluded from the heaven conjured by Blake. He portrays
these malefactors, their hands bound and chained, unable to embrace one another. By contrast, the blessed consist of lovers and
their offspring. "Men are admitted into heaven not because they
have curbed and governed their passions or have no passions,"
Blake insisted, "but because they have cultivated their under-
standings." Blake's amorous couples symbolized the uniting of
body and soul at the resurrection. Love attracts and combines; all
in heaven will be whole and complete.

In an echo from Germany, Friedrich Schiller, who wrote the
"Ode to Joy" that concludes Beethoven's Ninth Symphony, revived the Renaissance depiction of heaven as Elysium, where love
triumphs over death:

> *Here love finds the crown on earth denied her,*
> *And, death's threatening arm no more beside her,*
> *Keeps an endless wedding holiday!*

For Goethe, love had the power to both forgive and redeem. In
his heaven the unattainable

> *Here is realized;*
> *The Eternal Feminine*
> *Draws us upward.*

Goethe's imagination converts the patriarchal God of Christianity
into a yielding matriarch.

Robert Browning (1812–89), although happily married,
deemed marriage on earth to be "counterfeit," and reserved true

love for eternity: "In heaven we have the real and true and sure."
Lord Byron (1788–1824) viewed earthly marriage as a burden,
but in heaven "our chains once dissolved and our hearts uncon-
fined / We'll love without bonds, but we'll love you forever." In his
poem "If That High World" (1815), Byron pictured lovers in eternity seeking

> *To hold each heart the heart that shares;*
> *With them the immortal waters drink,*
> *And soul in soul grow deathless theirs!*

Heaven, originally reserved for divine contemplation, had become
home to human passion.

## *Calvaries of Love*

Before moving to Washington in the early seventies, I lived and
worked in Amherst, the small Massachusetts college town that
produced the sprightly poet Emily Dickinson (1830–86). At the
time, the chairman of Amherst College's religion department
rented the poet's home from the college for his family, on condition that he keep her room in authentic museum condition and allow tours one afternoon a week. I knew the house well, and once
even sat where Emily wrote her verse, wondering where the Belle
of Amherst got her inspiration.

The view from the poet's window is dominated now as during
her lifetime by a church; but the church did not rule Emily's
imagination. She rejected any heaven where "it's Sunday—all the
time" and joked that eternal rest would require "so many beds."

Although celibate throughout life, Dickinson believed passionate love would consume her afterlife, when she would finally
possess a man of her acquaintance whom she called Master, who

for some unexplained reason was unavailable to her in this life. Perhaps he was already married. Nevertheless, she pledged:

> *Sufficient troth, that we shall rise—*
> *Deposed—at length, the Grave—*
> *To that new marriage,*
> *Justified—through Calvaries of Love.*

In her verse, Dickinson also encounters Jesus in heaven, but the Savior's own face dissolves into the likeness of her earthly love:

> *The 'life that is to be,' to me*
> *A residence too plain*
> *Unless in my Redeemer's Face*
> *I recognize your own . . .*

In England, the Pre-Raphaelite poet-painter Dante Gabriel Rossetti improved on Blake's vision of heaven as the reunion of lovers. The heroine of "The Blessed Damozel" was no chaste medieval saint, but rather a ripe maiden for whom heaven was a misery while her lover was still on earth. She weeps because her other half is still mortal. Clearly, God is unable to make her whole; only a mortal man can do that.

While poets and artists did not much bother whether their imaginary lovers were married or not, churchmen looked to heaven to perpetuate and strengthen the marriage bond and family affection. To this end, they too embraced the new heaven of love. The German theologian Friedrich Schleiermacher pronounced himself persuaded that Adam, solitary in Paradise, was incapable of fully experiencing God. For that he required a woman, Eve, to provide love and community. In Schleiermacher's estimation, it was love that made religion possible.

Churchmen, both Protestant and Catholic, were careful not to challenge Jesus' revelation that "in the resurrection they neither marry, nor are given in marriage, but are as the angels of God in heaven" (Matthew 22:30). Nevertheless, straining to accommodate family and affection in eternity, they tinkered with the definition of marriage. For example, the American Calvinist Henry Harbaugh granted that marriage "in its earthly sense, comes to an end in death," but opined that "the relation in its mystical and spiritual sense continues, and its affections, beautiful and holy on earth, are made perfect and permanent in heaven." By equating marriage with reproductive intercourse, he conveniently confined it to earth, allowing for nonreproductive eternal love between the same spouses in heaven.

## Passion Versus Sentiment

What poets sought in heaven was perfect passion; what the church came to sanction was sentiment. But they used similar language and joined in preaching the primacy of affection. Charles Kingsley (1819–75), Queen Victoria's uxorious chaplain, pushed the envelope by insisting that heaven for him would consist of eternal conjugal union with his beloved wife, Fanny. Kingsley preached that passionate physical love between Christians could be chaste. "Those thrilling writhings are but dim shadows of a union which shall be perfect," he affirmed before his marriage. He agreed that there need be no marrying in heaven, *because he was already married,* ecstatically so. Fanny gushed agreement: "Beloved, if [Eve] shrank not, why sh'd I? If Holy Eden was the Scene of Marriage and Married Love, why should I fear to leap into your arms to realize one of Eden's blessings or taste an Enjoyment wh[ich] *must* be pure if it was *tasted* there."

While some shrank from an eternity of passion, most Christians by the second half of the nineteenth century favored an affectionate, domesticated heaven with family values. Elizabeth Stuart Phelps Ward's 1868 novel, *The Gates Ajar,* proved to be an international best-seller second in sales only to Harriet Beecher Stowe's *Uncle Tom's Cabin.* Mrs. Ward popularized the cozy Victorian heaven of eternal love, where she could expect "to have my beautiful home, and my husband and [child] as I had them here; with many differences and great ones, but mine just the same."

Ward's God was also domesticated as "a living Presence," and Jesus, she predicted, would be someone to talk with "as a man talketh with his friend." An unsentimental Mark Twain characterized Ward's afterlife as "a mean little ten-cent heaven about the size of Rhode Island." In *The Feminization of American Culture,* Ann Douglas agreed, dismissing the Victorian heaven as a "celestial retirement village."

Despite such criticism, the heaven of love and family would survive its critics in popular imagination until well into the twentieth century, when, under the influence of the Social Gospel, eternity would take on the note of service and become an earnest, even busier place.

Eventually, disillusioned by world wars, holocausts, and economic depressions, twentieth century Christians slackened their search for splendor in the grass and began to reconsider whether the old heaven of Augustine—"alone with the Alone"—might yet offer the only sure satisfaction of mankind's yearnings. Nevertheless, in anticipation of such a heaven, we will have to be prepared for surprises.

## Surprise!

It's safe to suggest that a puritan would be surprised (and chagrined) by a passionate and amatory heaven. So, too, would intellectuals, who prize their minds more than their emotions. If your idea of heaven on earth is to curl up on a couch with a six-pack in front of a TV set, you will be surprised and disappointed if heaven makes any demands on your energy. If you have dedicated your lifetime to service, you will be unpleasantly surprised if the principal activity of heaven is play.

Each of us wants heaven to preserve the values and to deliver the satisfactions we already cherish in life. In eternity many of us will seek rest from life's competitiveness and uncertainty, but you can be certain that Michael Jordan and his fellow athletes will be unhappy if not given a chance to compete—win or lose.

If heaven does no more than confirm and reward the values of a lifetime, then it is only a warranty extension, not the culmination and fulfillment of our lives. Eternity is unbounded by time, and heaven's gifts are not confined by our imaginations. Within our short lifetimes, not a single one of us explores more than a fraction of his or her potential for achievement and enjoyment. In heaven we will be all that we can be, limited only by God's imagination, which is infinite.

Most of life's blessings come as surprises. As a young man, I could not predict the woman who would share my life, the children who would expand it, the friends I would discover, or the careers I would follow. During the rare times when I thought I had my life securely planned, I invariably suffered *unpleasant* surprises—some of them temporary setbacks, but others outright failures. If we cannot predict the events of the next twenty-four hours, we surely cannot imagine the surprises eternity holds in store.

Nor should we be surprised if each person's heaven is somewhat different. Clearly, each of us is unique, and heaven is not a totalitarian state, ruled by God, whose residents must toe the identical line. If, as we are told, there are "many mansions" in heaven, there will be many satisfactions as well.

As I write, the residents of the nation's capital await the results of a lottery whose winner will pocket $250 million. As people stood in long lines to purchase tickets, reporters asked scores of them how they would spend that astronomical sum to make themselves happy. No respondent could account for spending more than a few million dollars to purchase the good life—mansions, yachts, fashions, jewelry, and travel. After that, their imaginations ran out.

Only our Creator and designer has the imagination to know what complete happiness will be for each of us, and only he can deliver it. But some things appear certain. God is love, so it's safe to predict that there will be intimacy in heaven. But will it be only friendship and affection, or passion as well?

Mystics of all religious traditions have reported their ecstasies in terms that suggest sensuality. However, since the human vocabulary of sensation is limited, it's wise not to jump to the conclusion that we will engage in sexual relations in heaven. God, the subject and object of the mystics' ardor, is hardly a sexual partner. Moreover, since there is no need for reproduction in eternity, sexuality as we know it seems pointless in heaven.

If we are to credit the mystics, ecstasy in eternity will stem directly from God and only indirectly from our intimacy with one another. Human sexuality is possessive, exclusive, and emotionally restrictive. In eternity, earthly lovers will still love one another more intimately and ardently, but not to the exclusion of others. Heaven will be a democracy of affection.

Beyond those few timid predictions, I am ready for surprises.

# EIGHT

# YOU ARE LEAVING NOTHING BEHIND

Keep your treasure in Heaven where there is
neither moth nor rust to spoil it, and nobody
can break in and steal. For wherever your
treasure is . . . your heart will be there too!

MATTHEW 6:20–21

The Epistle of Diognetus, composed in the second century, characterized the early Christians as exiles on earth because they were citizens of heaven. The earliest Christians lived in imminent expectation of the end of life as we know it. For them, eternity had already begun. Their lives exemplified Saint Paul's conviction that "for me, to live is Christ and to die is gain" (Philippians 1:21).

The blind poet John Milton anticipated his demise as "the golden key that opens the palace of eternity." His countryman John Donne wrote with conviction that "I shall not live 'till I see God; and when I have seen Him, I shall never die."

Our own American poet Walt Whitman exulted in the prospect of eternity:

**Our life is closed, our life begins . . .**
**Joy, shipmate, joy!**

But how can we find joy when, on dying, we leave everything we love behind us? The Quaker colonist William Penn
answers: "They that love beyond the world cannot be separated by it. Death cannot kill what never dies, nor can spirits ever be divided that love and live in the same divine
principle."

ℬ

ONCE WE CROSS the border into eternity, our survivors may
weep for losing us temporarily, but we will have no cause to
mourn for them or for ourselves. Whatever we have pawned in
this life we will redeem in the next. Whatever we may have lost
we will find—in abundance.

There is an unresolved dispute in Christian theology whether
the dead are able to pray for the living, but it is agreed that the
living can pray for the dead. When the wind is blowing into
Washington from Arlington National Cemetery, pedestrians on
the city's busy streets can hear the crack of rifles across the Po-
tomac honoring another compatriot laid to rest. The prayers pronounced at the grave site are not loud enough to carry to the
capital, but they reach God.

C. S. Lewis suggests that God eternally takes into account
everything that happens in time. If that is true, then even before
he created time, God knew we would pray. Our prayers, even
those we have not as yet uttered, have been weighed in the balance
eternally. Of course, only God comprehends how prayer can have
any effect, but it can be no more mysterious than love, which defies measurement but transforms life.

People of faith pray with confidence that their next life will be better than this one, but also that they will lose nothing that they have loved, learned, and accomplished this side of heaven. By its very nature, time is limited in what it can contain of joy. The happiness of this moment will surely recede. But eternity contains all the moments of time, and more. Its promise is infinite. Not only will we leave nothing behind in time; we will gain everything in eternity. That is where our treasure is, and where our hearts should be even now.

Of course, those who believe that life ends in decay expect to lose everything at death. But those, also, who believe that life never ends but is merely renewed in an endless series of reincarnations leave everything behind. More than one-fifth of the world's people believe that time itself is endless and that death is not the passageway to eternity, but only to yet another finite lifetime on this earth. Buddhists, Hindus, Theosophists, and many others hold that each of us, after death, is reincarnated as another creature, with no memory of his or her former life. All that remains from the previous life is its merit, which affects the quality of the new life. Everything else— one's identity, personality, memory, knowledge, accomplishment, experience, and affection—is abandoned in rebirth.

According to reincarnationists, a child born today into comfortable circumstances, with gifts of intellect, taste, and compassion, is presumed to have merited this reward because of a previous, unremembered life that was conducted virtuously. In their estimation, rewards and punishments are meted out in time, not in eternity. A unfortunate person can only assume his present condition is punishment for his vices in an earlier existence. But he will never know, because he is now another person altogether, and cannot even recall the faults of his former self.

## *Where Is Justice in the Universe?*

The possibility of reincarnation is routinely (and often airily) dismissed by theologians in the West, where faith in rebirth finds refuge mainly among spiritualists, but increasingly among converts to Buddhism. In the East, it is altogether a different matter: reincarnation is woven into the fabric of faith and culture. Moreover, the notion of rebirth is common among present-day primitive peoples on every continent, possibly because it answers (more convincingly even than Christianity) the core question, where is justice in the universe?

In Judaism, Christianity, and Islam, each individual life is regarded as a one-act play: one is born at a certain time and place in favorable or abject circumstances that affect health, education, and nurturing. The Budweiser beer commercial claims that "you only go round once in life," which pretty well sums up conventional thinking in the Western world. In religious terms, each of us is expected in a single brief span to prove himself or herself worthy of spending eternity with God. According to Western beliefs, when we die, we leave nothing behind, retaining our identity, our memories, our accomplishments, and our loves throughout eternity. In some sense we will be better persons in eternity, but we will be the same persons. Oddly, many Westerners are drawn to the notion of reincarnation but fail to reflect that, in rebirth, they would lose everything from their current lives, including their sense of self. In each rebirth they would become somebody else altogether.

So what is the appeal of endless time on earth over eternal life in heaven? Only this: reincarnation appears to deal better than Western faiths with the injustices of life. As we discovered in Catholicism's perceived need to contrive a purgatory to make sense of our destiny, the conventional script of Western faith leaves loose ends. In reality, people don't make seamless successes and failures of their lives. The lives most of us lead are inconsistent morally, and occasionally a complete muddle. Moreover, each of us is impeded or assisted unevenly and unfairly by circumstances. How can anyone be expected to live a life of love if that person is born sick and impoverished and is afforded no education? Contrariwise, how can a wicked person who has victimized hundreds of persons throughout life pull off a deathbed conversion, have a messy slate wiped clean, and be absorbed eternally in Abraham's bosom? As Broadway's mythical king of Siam was wont to exclaim: " 'Is a puzzlement!"

The three great religions that sprang from the Middle East are inclined to leave the quandary to God—an inclination supported by our shared conviction that there is a personal God who has our best interests at heart. We trust God to iron out the inequities, ensuring that we lose nothing of value that we have gained in this life, while adding the gift of eternity. But in the East, religious faith lays claim to no loving Father, no dying Son, no abiding Spirit to direct its teeming masses into eternity.

Instead, the faithful solve the riddle of destiny by invoking fate—an inexorable, impersonal design that decrees a crude justice, but justice nonetheless. Life driven by fate is an endless play, with a person's birth and death marking only the curtain's rise and fall for but one act. The next act begins immediately with the actor in a new body, place, and role, determined by how well he or she performed in the last. Were you high, mighty, and cruel in your previous life? Then in your next you may be brought low, but you will not thereby elude fate, which will judge you once again and determine your subsequent reincarnation.

Not surprisingly, in Buddhist and Hindu cultures there is a temptation to regard less fortunate persons without compassion or intervention. This stems from the assumption that the poverty and misery of others may simply be fate's punishment for evil in their earlier lives. Of course, in its impersonal way, fate also rewards good, so life is not just a long-shot lottery but an investment in a better life next time around. Aside from imposing a rough justice, reincarnation also solves the dilemma of Western religions about what happens to the soul immediately after death: it enters a new body.

Roughly two-thirds of the world's population believes in reincarnation, though not necessarily as an official tenet of their religious faith. Surprisingly, nearly one-fourth of Americans also believe in rebirth, despite the fact that many of them are members of churches that explicitly reject the notion. Why? Transmigration is an accessory they have added uncritically to their chosen creed, and with typical American optimism, they expect their next reincarnation will be better than their present one. For people uncomfortable with the notion of spending eternity with a God they do not know, reincarnation can seem to be an attractive alternative.

## *The Draw of Reincarnation*

The idea of reincarnation boasts a respectable history. The ancient Greeks Pythagoras and Plato were both believers in successive lives. In fact, Plato (c. 427–347 B.C.) opined that, were it not for this succession, life in the universe would cease altogether. In ancient Egypt it was believed that great souls were reincarnated from generation to generation as leaders of the nation; in time, the notion of rebirth was expanded to include the masses as well. The Egyptian Book of the Dead includes prayer formulas aimed at encouraging favorable reincarnation.

Primitive cultures in the contemporary world continue to cling to this belief. Among some African tribes, childlessness is considered a curse, because they believe new bodies are needed as homes for reborn souls. Among Pacific Island cultures, belief in rebirth is common on Bali, Okinawa, Tasmania, Fiji, New Caledonia, in Melanesia and the Solomon Islands, as well as among the Ainu in northern Japan and the Maoris of New Zealand. In Australia, aborigines of the shrinking central tribes poignantly aspire to be reborn as "white fellows" in their future lives.

Rebirth is also woven into the fabric of faith among many native North American tribes. In Alaska, the Tlingits believe that a soul speaks to each pregnant woman in her dreams, announcing its intent to be reincarnated through her. At birth, the child's likely previous lives must be ascertained so it can take credit for the good it did in its earlier incarnations. Among the Tlingits, the biological mother and father are credited only with providing a new body for a soul that has already lived a multitude of lifetimes.

Ironically, the Spanish conquest and Christianization of what is now Latin America was assisted by the natives' belief in reincarnation. When the conquistadors arrived, they were mistaken for reborn gods—Quetzalcoatl in Mexico and Viracocha in Peru—and vast native populations placed themselves reverently at the mercy of these rapacious visitors, who were all too human.

Although reincarnation is ultimately alien to Islam and Judaism, allusions to rebirth can be found in their literature of faith. Muhammad was influenced by the ancient Persian belief in rebirth, as well as by Zoroastrianism. Transmigration is explicit in *The Desatir,* a mystical work completed not long before the Prophet embarked on his career. Some scholars find allusions to reincarnation in the Koran, for example: "He sent down rain from above in proper quantity and he brings back to life the dead earth, similarly ye shall be reborn" (chapter 25—Meccan verses 5-10-6). But this could be interpreted equally as a reference to resurrection. Esoteric schools of Islam variously cling to beliefs in the periodic incarnation of the Perfect Man, or God-man, and the rebirth of the Imam (a divinity originally thought to be manifested in the Prophet himself), as well as in the transmigration of ordinary souls.

In Judaism, there is no direct reference to reincarnation in the Torah. However, the Kabbalah, a medieval compendium of mystical books of esoteric rabbinical teaching, mentions the process (described, in Hebrew, as *gilgul*). In our day, rebirth finds some resonance among Hasidic Jews but is spurned by the three principal branches of Judaism: Orthodox, Conservative, and Reform. The Kabbalah argued that the earliest Jews believed in the rebirth of great prophets: Adam into David into the Messiah. In later centuries, kabbalist Jews speculated that individual souls are only the shattered remnants of the souls of the first man, Adam.

## The Wheel of Rebirth

Reincarnation is a central tenet of Hinduism, the prominent faith of India, whose population is fast approaching a billion people. As soon as he or she can understand, every Hindu child is taught that this new life is merely the latest of the soul's many existences, and hardly his or her last. Hinduism holds that samsara, the wheel of rebirth, revolves relentlessly because of faults in the soul. It is driven by both ignorance and desire. Escape from the endless play is unlikely but conceivable should the soul in its current incarnation manage to achieve self-knowledge and purge itself utterly of earthly passion.

Karma, the inflexible law of cause and effect, does not guarantee justice during one's present life, but only in the next. Therefore, if I am good this time around, I will be accorded a better life next time; if I abuse my present incarnation, I may be reborn in abysmal circumstances or in less-than-human form. Hindus believe the soul enjoys brief respites between its rebirths, allowing it to reflect on its progress or regress.

In Hindu literature, the notion of reincarnation can be traced to the Vedas, sacred writings dating back to a millennium before the birth of Christ. The concept is further elaborated in the Bhagavadgita, the song of the Lord Krishna, composed between 400 B.C. and A.D. 200. Krishna, who is considered by Hindus to be the eighth incarnation of a god, proclaims the self to be eternal: "Both I and thou have passed through many births! Mine are known to me, but thou knowest not of thine." Hindus believe that with constant effort through successive lives, the soul can gain release from its bondage to the flesh and attain peace, rest, and grace at last in Brahmin, the Absolute.

## Buddhism

Better known in the West than Hinduism, Buddhism borrows its notion of rebirth from the older faith. But according to its tenets, rebirth is not the same as reincarnation. Originally, Buddha taught that every man and woman possesses both a lesser self, which dies with the body, and a greater self, which survives. But as the Buddhist faith evolved, it came to teach that no ego passes intact from life to life. Rather, one's soul shatters at death and new personalities are formed from the fragments of broken souls. What survives intact is the life force, ruled by karma and perpetuated by the "three unwholesome roots"—desire, delusion, and hatred. If these internal enemies can be conquered, one may attain the deliverance of nirvana, which is defined at once as extinction and enlightenment.

According to Buddhism, a creature can expect to be reborn in any of six states, ranging from hell to heaven, as that person seeks to purge evil. But even the more sought after incarnations are only temporary. Rising to the status of a god, while favorable, is not a permanent escape from the relentlessly turning wheel of rebirth. And only in the human state is a man or woman capable of being conscious of the possibility of deliverance and setting one's course for escape. The alternatives are awful: one can rise provisionally to the character of a god or elemental force, but can topple into rebirth as a beast, a ghost, or a denizen of hell, utterly unaware of what it might take to escape this new stage.

Dying correctly is critical to both Hinduism and Buddhism, because both faiths posit that one's final thought in life is instrumental in defining the next incarnation. Accordingly, it is imperative that one prepare well for death, which is perceived not as immediate extinction but as a progressive loss of consciousness over a period extending as long as four days, followed by an after-death transition to rebirth that (according to the Tibetan Book of the Dead) extends for another forty-nine days.

## Rebirth in Christianity and in Literature

There have been spotty attempts to introduce the notion of reincarnation into Christianity, beginning with the first major heresy, Gnosticism. Although John the Baptist rejected allegations that he was the reincarnation of the prophet Elijah, an ancient Coptic manuscript discovered in 1945 alleges that Jesus himself confided John's identity as Elijah to Mary Magdalen. The ancient church fathers Justin Martyr and Origen both believed in the preexistence of the soul, which theoretically would allow for the possibility of successive incarnations.

Rebirth has always enjoyed a fashion among those who believe in the existence of a hidden body of wisdom protected from the masses of believers. In contrast, mainstream Christianity insists that revelation is open and complete—that every believer possesses everything necessary to work out his or her salvation. Nevertheless, reincarnation was favored in the Middle Ages by elitist Christian cults, including the Cathars and Albigenses, the

Knights Templar, and the Rosicrucians. The notion survives to the present day in the tenets of Freemasonry. Among contemporary Christian denominations, only the Unity Church explicitly preaches reincarnation, yet interprets it as a regeneration or purification that comes to a conclusion.

Popular literature abounds in speculation about the transmigration of souls. Contemporary Theosophists and spiritualists borrow encouragement from the giants of German philosophy and literature—Kant, Lessing, Goethe, and Schopenhauer among them, each of whom flirted with reincarnation. For example, in his *Education of the Human Race,* Lessing mused: "Why should I not return as often as I am sent, to acquire new knowledge and new skills? Do I take away so much at one go that it is not worth the effort to come again?"

Nietzsche confessed to a terrifying experience, not of successive births but of the eternal recurrence of the *same* life. He died insane. His frightening dream was poignantly dramatized in the 1993 film *Groundhog Day,* in which the protagonist awakens each morning to the identical series of events he encountered the day before. Every new day is the same as yesterday; life's script never changes a comma. Predictably, Hollywood manages a happy ending. Our hero discovers that he can alter from day to day the way he deals with the same set of circumstances and people. By confronting the same challenges more intelligently and humanely, he is ultimately redeemed and returned to real time. Of course, that is the Hollywood version; Nietzsche feared that no such escape from recurrence might be possible.

### Reincarnation Reconsidered

Reincarnation is unpopular in the Western world because it runs contrary to the prevailing optimism that we can improve the quality of life from generation to generation. Impoverished societies may find every day the same, but in industrialized societies we are strivers, worshiping novelty and change.

At first blush, the transmigration of souls seems to explain why bad things happen to good people—because of evil wrought in a former life. Rebirth also appears to offer a crude justice in life for everyone, promising more joy or misery in our next incarnation according to the good or evil we accomplish in the present.

Reincarnation is compatible with belief in a relentless, impersonal fate ruling the universe. Reincarnation is incompatible with the belief of Christians, Jews, and Moslems in a personal Creator who has our eternal interests at heart. If eternal rebirth is necessary, God is vulnerable to the accusation that he botched our creation at the outset. To put it another way, reincarnation is equivalent to an auto maker's warranty that keeps our car going back again and again for repairs because of defects in its original manufacture. Rebirth is an infinite product recall.

Hindus agree that an infinite series of rebirths having no beginning makes no sense. If every man, woman, and child now alive can trace all his or her existences to an original life, we are confronted with the question, what accounts for the failure the first time around that made all these subsequent lives necessary? Again, our Creator is the logical culprit. Why, being God, didn't he get it right the first time? Christians, Jews, and Moslems reply that God didn't fail his creatures; his creatures failed him.

If so, it makes the Genesis story of the generous Creator and the presumptuous creature worth a second look. In the beginning God didn't get it wrong; man and woman did. But God didn't perpetuate our error eternally; he offered redemption to each creature individually, sending his own Son to become human to show every person how to get life right the first (and only) time around.

Moreover, reincarnation assumes that a fully formed soul enters into a new body, as a hermit crab scuttles to lay claim to an empty shell as its home. But experience suggests that each human being is formed by nature and nurture from infancy, if not from the womb. I not only *look* like my parents; I have inherited their strengths and weaknesses. I am predisposed temperamentally and behaviorally because I am *their* offspring, not an alien soul inhabiting an available body.

Simple addition illustrates that reincarnation cannot be the general rule. At this moment there are more people alive on earth than at any given time in the past, and the world's population has been expanding. We cannot all be reincarnations of persons who died just before each of us was born, because there weren't enough people alive then. Look back even farther through generations, centuries, and millennia, and there are even fewer candidates to ensure us all previous lives. If reincarnation has any credibility, it is as an exception, not a rule.

## Past Lives

Years ago, as an undergraduate in psychology, I witnessed fellow students under hypnosis revert to earlier stages in their lives. When they were pressed far enough, their emotions, voices, and expressions became infantile. They were, however, reporting on the same life. But under hypnosis, some men and women change personality altogether, exemplifying the behavior and speech of persons that may have lived in the past. Do these cases argue for reincarnation?

Psychologist Roger Woolger uses regression therapy to help his patients confront physical and mental dysfunction. Dr. Woolger discovers that patients sometimes take refuge in former lives because their present lives are intolerable. He acknowledges that these past lives may be only metaphors, but if they help patients to confront present needs, he encourages their exploration. However, he discourages his patients from wallowing in the past, in favor of confronting their present lives.

Dr. Brian Weiss, chairman of the Department of Psychiatry at Mt. Sinai Medical Center in Miami, is also skeptical of the historicity of past lives, but he has successfully treated patients suffering from near emotional paralysis by distancing them from their current trauma and resolving their problems by assuming a more stable personality, setting aside the question of whether that personality comes from a previous life.

Past-life regression appears to be a therapy useful for resolving present dysfunction, not a demonstration of rebirth. The technique is not unlike dealing with multiple personality disorders, where successful therapy establishes the dominance of a healthy, responsible ego over weaker, destructive personalities. We often become stronger ourselves by reference to a real hero or role model from the past, but it does not follow that we are that person's reincarnation.

Reports of former lives under hypnosis or medication are susceptible to suggestion. In recent years, an increasing number of well-intentioned therapists have suggested to children that they have been abused by adults, only to be censured by the courts for putting those ideas in the children's heads. Therapists have also been maligned for encouraging sufferers of multiple personality disorders to believe in those "other selves" and to add even more.

But if reincarnation is not the rule, could it be a rare exception? In extensive research conducted over more than three decades, Dr. Ian Stevenson, professor of psychiatry at the University of Virginia Medical School, has studied over two thousand children in India, Sri Lanka, Brazil, and Lebanon, as well as among the Tlingit Indians in Alaska. No hypnosis is involved. Typically, the children report detailed recollections of an earlier existence that they could not be expected to know in their present lives. These spontaneous memories fade after a few years, but they include intimate details of the lives of real people recently deceased. Admittedly, the cultures into which these children are born favor belief in reincarnation. Nevertheless, no one appears to be lying or to have any cause for pretense.

Stevenson is careful to state that his studies are only "suggestive" of transmigration. Nevertheless, in 1975 the *Journal of the American Medical Association* noted that Dr. Stevenson "had collected cases in which the evidence is difficult to explain on any other grounds" than reincarnation.

## *Justice and Forgiveness*

The justice that reincarnation appears to offer rests on our being fully conscious of what is at stake morally as we each attempt to improve our lot and ultimately escape the wheel of rebirth. But in fact, few of us are aware of previous incarnations. Whatever credence one is tempted to give to accounts of past-life regression, it is a rare phenomenon and no help to the billions of men, women, and children who must muddle through life this very day with their own personalities.

A genuinely moral universe presupposes a life *after* the present one, *not before*. Moreover, the virtues of justice and moral effort that render reincarnation appealing are already contained in Christianity. Our next life will reflect the reverence we show our present life. But there is no need for the cycle to go on and on. If, as seems likely, most people's behavior over their life spans is less than exemplary, that is no justification for starting over from scratch again and again.

If the only justice you and I can count on in the universe is meted out by a relentless and unfeeling fate, what is the point of morality at all? *Who's* to care? Here Christians, Jews, and Moslems all answer in chorus: *God* cares. Reincarnation assumes that the slate is wiped clean after each life as one starts all over again. But that ignores the presence of love and insults the progress of civilization. The world that each new infant enters is the product of the successes and failings of countless previous persons. As Abraham Lincoln affirmed, "We cannot escape history."

If life is indeed the legacy, in part, of the failings of countless generations, then what the universe needs is not to trash the past and to start over. Rather, what it requires is forgiveness for the past, grace for the present, and hope for the future. That is what fate cannot provide but God does. Endless rebirth and consequent loss of our selves is not the answer. Rather, we will move on to our Creator, taking everything of value with us, leaving nothing behind. God will be our reward.

# NINE

# YOU HAVE BEEN PREPARING FOR ETERNITY ALL YOUR LIFE

*To die will be an awfully big adventure.*

J. M. BARRIE, *PETER PAN*

Vance Havner often confided, "I'm homesick for heaven." The prospect of heaven infused daily significance into the evangelist's life. He welcomed death as the portal to eternity.

As never before, the signs of eternity surround us. In the past, history was consigned to dustbins and heroes to their graves. Today, through film and videotape, we have conferred a virtual immortality on persons who have long since departed this life.

When they were very young, my daughters often pointed to the TV screen and asked, "Is that person alive?" Even adults can be permitted some confusion. On any given weekend, television brings us Marilyn Monroe, John Wayne, James Dean, and a constellation of stars whose lights have never dimmed. The majority of the recordings I enjoy are by artists who have long since departed this life. I have seen the Astaire-Rogers films countless times and reckon the dancing pair to be more alive than I often feel. My wife and I named our two new kittens Fred and Ginger to keep that lively couple's memory alive in our home.

Poets have long been counseled to die young so they will be remembered for their youth and vitality. But the fabric of life is all of one piece, now and hereafter. By living in the light of heaven, we will enter eternity youthful and ready for adventure.

ℬↄ

WHEREAS CYNICS CONCEIVE OF LIFE as a countdown to death and suicides seek nothing better than oblivion, Christians embrace the present life as nothing less than the overture to eternity. In the economy of salvation, as in physics, nothing is lost; it is only transformed. The infinitesimal atom that is now compost may one day be in a brain cell of the next Einstein. The lives we now lead—with whatever misgivings and handicaps—will never truly end. Instead, they will be merely transfigured. Your death will make a difference, but it will not make *you* different. In eternity, it is fair to predict that you will be more yourself than ever before. Were you funny in life? You will be hilarious in heaven. Were you a terror? You will be terrible in eternity.

When I consult my stiff joints on awakening each morning and fuss over the proliferation of pills in my medicine cabinet, I am defining life as a process of growing old. Fair enough: as economist John Maynard Keynes acknowledged, "In the long run we're all dead." Nevertheless, speaking for myself, I still sense a twenty-year-old struggling to get out of this antique shell I drag around. As a Christian, I am persuaded that death does not end life but is only a transaction that will allow me to trade in this old model for one that is better equipped for eternity. It is a prospect to which we devote our lives, and it helps us prepare for the final moments this side of eternity.

## Life in the Light of Eternity

During their lifetimes, some farsighted Americans, seeking to spare their loved ones the expense of disposing of their remains, arrange to purchase plots and headstones; some of them even pre-pay the mortician for their final sweep from dust to dust. As the old saw affirms, the only sure things in this world are death and taxes; and while the taxman visits frequently, the Grim Reaper puts in but a single appearance. One should be prepared.

A journalist of my acquaintance has made even further arrangements. She has erected a monument to herself in a Washington cemetery and arranged for the details and sentiments she considers to best characterize her life to be carved into a massive headstone. Unlike most of us, she has composed her own epitaph, and needless to say, it is complimentary. Celebrities who publish their memoirs late in life similarly seek to carve literary headstones in the form of self-serving autobiographies.

For a long time, I suspected friends who devour the obituaries in the daily paper of possessing a morbid streak, but their sheer numbers have forced me to reconsider my judgment and to sneak a look myself at the death notices before concentrating on the sports and editorial pages. Because of the pressure of deadlines and the unpredictability of events, journalism is a sometimes slapdash enterprise, its daily practitioners producing something this side of literature. The exception is the largely anonymous worldwide corps of obituary writers, who, as historians before the fact, enjoy the leisure of critiquing the lives of persons still living, in full confidence that the only flourishes that will need to be added before their stories' appearance is a sentence about the time, place, and cause of death. Compared to reporters who on occasion risk life and limb pursuing stories their editors may never run, the obituary writer knows that with patience (and in complete safety), his effort will eventually see print.

An English friend confides that he is the author of the obituary of Ronald Reagan that will run in the *Independent* when our former actor-president leaves to meet his ultimate producer-director. My friend reshapes and updates the piece from time to time in heady confidence that, when the piece is printed, its subject will be in no position to object to anything in it.

Years ago, when my wife and I were impoverished newlyweds, we moonlighted as counselors to people who wanted to get ahead in their careers or change jobs altogether. Rather than teach them the mechanics of writing a résumé, we asked them to compose their own obituaries—an exercise in assessing their lives to date and predicting their futures—noting their achievements and failures and uncovering their priorities in life. The resulting compositions revealed that many of our clients weren't simply looking for raises and promotions. Rather they found themselves mired in unfulfilling lines of work. Their real virtues, abilities, and aspirations were utterly unrelated to earning a living. In composing their obituaries they began to discover what their lives stood for and what mattered to them.

### Instant Analysis

You can accomplish the shorthand equivalent of writing your epitaph if you will answer, hastily and without reflection, the question, who am I? (No cheating now! Once you hesitate, thinking before you answer, you are tidying up the truth and will lose the revelation.) To illustrate, allow me to serve as guinea pig.

*Who am I?* "I am David Yount, a man, a husband, father, American, Christian, writer, homebody, lover of animals and all things beautiful." I could chatter on and on, of course, but I note that I falter ever so slightly at this point, so by our rules the game is over. Let's see what I have revealed to myself about myself, on the theory that these are my actual priorities at the moment. Surely my answer illustrates that my personal life comes first, but heavy laden with complacency. I didn't, for instance, toss in adjectives such as "loving" or "faithful" or "devoted." My answer suggests that I seem to have some need to assert gender and jingoism. I neglected to mention anything about being a friend or an employer, and nothing at all about the way I earn my living or about my responsibilities to the community beyond my hearth. On reflection, I wish I thought of myself as a friend and a good citizen. On the other hand, I appear not to be burdened by defining myself according to appearance, education, health, accomplishment, wealth, or taste—all admittedly fragile things. Matters could be worse with my self-image. I have heard people answer the question, who are you? with a single affirmation that was a negation: "I'm a loser." "I am unattractive." "I'm hopeless." Even when one's retort is confident ("I'm gay," "I'm a patriot," "I'm a liberal"), these proud self-concepts can be stiflingly restrictive. For our own sakes, we could be so much more.

By the time you read this, my five-cent self-psychoanalysis will probably reveal revised priorities—more generous ones, I hope. In any case, I commend this occasional exercise to you on the principle that each of us is likely to prize in eternity what he or she values now.

## *Celebrating Life, Anticipating Eternity*

In the better British newspapers, obituary writing has developed into something of an art form, celebrating lives rather than mourning their passing. The *Economist* notes that "obituary writers tend to be unhappy at even the suggestion that their work has anything to do with death as such—beyond its necessary role as a peg for publication." These days a well-written obituary does not concentrate on what the deceased left behind, but on what he or she contributed in life. What we stand for and value in this life is what we carry into the next.

In his book *When All You've Ever Wanted Isn't Enough,* Rabbi Harold Kushner argues that the only permanent satisfaction acquisitiveness can offer is the possession of a life that has meaning. If there is any literal truth to the notion that heaven is a neighborhood composed of "many mansions," each individual resident is also the architect, builder, and landscaper of his own heavenly housing. Eternity is not simply an extended run of the play we have been acting all our lives. Rather, it is our big chance: taking our act to Broadway. In eternity, our names will be in lights. The critical question is, how good is our act? Far from being an indulgence of Walter Mittyish fantasies, our afterlife will be the realization of the realities we have valued and to which we have devoted ourselves in good times and bad this side of the great divide.

I suspect the afterlife is like a paid-up mortgage. You will still enjoy the same house with all its comforts and peculiarities, but now no one can evict you—the result of your years of investing in it. If God makes me welcome, I predict that my own mansion in eternity will be as small or large and as well or poorly maintained as my life has been. To mix metaphors, if the world is your oyster, then you will not want for seafood in eternity. If, on the other hand, you have huddled for safety in a life no bigger than the closet of your own tiny thoughts and feelings, you will likely find your accommodations in eternity equally cramped.

Until recently, obituary writers followed the dictum *De mortuis nihil nisi bonum* (don't say anything about the dead unless you can say something good). This is not unlike the physician's Hippocratic oath to do no harm. True to that constraint, obits in the past took the form of funeral elegies (for example, "Although never one to suffer fools gladly, he was untiring in his charitable works, devotion to family, and love of animals").

What is new in contemporary journalism is that the "fools" the deceased suffered during life now want their fifteen minutes of celebrity to let the world know what they thought of the pompous old boy or girl. The new rule is that the frankness of the appreciation should match, but not exceed, the candor with which the subject conducted himself or herself in life. If you are a guarded person in life, your privacy will probably be respected, but your demise may go unheralded.

My late mother, who in her prefeminist work life toiled as a poorly paid stenographer, composed a brief obituary before her death, in her eighties, indulging in innocent revisionism, claiming a career as an "administrative assistant." I plead guilty to sly revisionism myself, using a photo on the dustcover that depicts me nearly a decade more youthful than my mirror reveals. Poets who die young (Keats, Owen) will, alas, always be young, whereas poets who die old will be remembered as codgers (Tennyson, Whitman, Frost, and Sandburg come to mind), even when their best work was produced in their youthful years.

But regardless of how we are remembered, we do not earn our salvation by impressing anyone—be it God, the public, or even ourselves—but by devoting ourselves to values we can carry into eternity.

## Embracing the Executioner

In a time both crueler and more courteous than our own, inmates in the Tower of London were expected not only to pay room and board to their jailers during their captivity but to compensate their executioners for dispatching them into eternity. In addition, the hangman and axe man were entitled to their victims' clothing, jewelry, and accessories—an echo of Jesus' executioners casting lots for his cloak as he hung on the cross.

To contemporary sensibilities, the very mention of capital punishment is repugnant. So what are we to make of the fact that not so long ago it was expected that the condemned forgive and embrace the hooded wielder of axe and noose—and indeed, to pray for his executioner? The answer, I believe, reveals more than quaintness or grisly good manners; it strikes to the heart of what believers then affirmed about life and death.

To illustrate: Thomas More, like many in his time, was executed for what we would call political reasons. He had become an inconvenience to Henry VIII, whom he had served as chancellor. At the time, public executions served the ruler's purposes as displays of naked power—not least the power to intimidate. Unlike the covert state executions of our own day, these very public displays were intended to set an example and uphold the public order. Requested according to protocol to pardon the axe man, More embraced his executioner, assuring him that they both shared the same fate. The only difference was that More was being dispatched on his final journey sooner.

Though More's final gestures may strike us as high drama, they only conveyed a confidence commonly held among Christians of the time. Victims and spectators alike shared a common belief: that their lives were a gift from God, and that death (however encountered) was but a passage from this life to another—hopefully a better one. There was no presumption that being condemned to death was a ticket to perdition. The mass murderer and the victim whose only crime was to have been politically incorrect were ultimately subject to the judgment not of government but of their consciences and their Maker. Unlike the state, God was known to be in a permanently forgiving mood.

In all likelihood you and I will not depart life on the gallows—or in any way prematurely. But whereas many people are stoic about the prospect of death, few of us meet it with the equanimity, hope, and lightheartedness of legions of earlier believers, both grand and simple, who met their own deaths violently before their allotted time. A smile at the end is better than a stiff upper lip.

Our contemporary reluctance to appreciate the promise of eternity stems largely from an aversion to facing the fact of death—which perverts a natural process into something to be feared. The denial of death is a very recent phenomenon, and not a good one. As a child raised in the ethnic neighborhoods of Chicago, I was accustomed to witnessing death in the stockyards and packing houses. But my lingering recollection is of the funeral homes where we mourned the latest neighborhood patriarch or matriarch to have departed life.

In our neighborhood, three and sometimes four generations of the same family lived cramped together in the same apartments, and the dying were tended at home, rather than in hospitals and nursing homes. Therefore death, when it came, was something that literally visited the home, and it was only natural that the Polish, Czech, and Irish families of my youth should hold wakes there. Caskets were open for viewing, and no one conceived of reducing Grandpa's or Grandma's body to ashes in an urn. While the surviving adults and children sorrowed over their loss, they treated death as a final rite of passage and a consummation of a life of fidelity, full of hope. No one dwelled on death; nothing about these occasions was morbid. Everything was natural.

## The Fear of Death

The fear of death is misplaced. One can be *anxious,* for example, about debt, illness, unemployment, or the loss of love, attractiveness, and reputation because (1) these misfortunes are uncertain and (2) they hurt in anticipation as well as in experience. By contrast, death is certain, and as we noted at the outset, it does not hurt.

The prospect of eternity is fulfillment, not loss. It is the living who sense loss when a loved one or leader dies. The cliché at every wake is the inevitable observation that the deceased looks peaceful. It is a cliché precisely because it is true: the dead do not grieve at all and have only passed through death to new life. It is those of us who remain who grieve our loss.

More often than not, the dying are ready to die, whether they are accident victims, children with cancer, young people with AIDS, or the aged, whose tired bodies have long since lost their warranty. It is their loved ones who are not prepared to lose them. In *A Grief Observed,* C. S. Lewis poignantly chronicled the loss of his wife to cancer. The most optimistic of men, possessed of an ability to discern sense in tragedy and to rationalize absurdity, Lewis found himself devastated by his personal loss. If you recall his story from the film *Shadowlands,* however, you will remember that his wife was actually prepared for death. She was true to her given name—Joy—to the end.

When I was a seminarian disputing over things theological, the theoretical question was debated whether death is natural or rather a punishment for original sin. If one literally accepts the biblical admonition that "the wages of sin is death," then you and I are paying for mistakes made in Eden. But Jesus rejected the notion that death is anyone's fault. When his antagonists demanded whether the blind and lame were being punished for their own sins or for those of their parents, he answered: *neither*. Sickness simply happens. Then Jesus proceeded to cure their maladies. Death, which discomfits one's survivors, is neither punishment nor an ending for the deceased, but only the passage to a different kind of life.

Of course, I am speaking here only of death itself, not of dying, which can be protracted, painful, and degrading. When he was my age, my father had already been forced to retire because of the degenerating effects of arteriosclerosis. Over the final twenty-one years of his life, he progressively lost his mental and physical faculties. Death, when it finally visited him, was deliverance. So, too, was my mother's passing a few years later. The only child of blind parents, raised on public welfare and private charity, she became embittered when the golden years for which she had toiled turned to rust. She died, immobile and bedridden after a series of illnesses, persuaded that life had cheated her, but confident of a better eternity.

## Best of All Possible Worlds?

I mention these personal sorrows to reassure the reader that I am no Pollyanna about life and death. Voltaire's Dr. Pangloss preached that this is the best of all possible worlds, but I protest that I can think of many possible improvements. All three of my daughters were born learning disabled, with sensory-motor deficits that render ordinary activities extraordinarily difficult to accomplish. In a better world they would function without these hardships. When Jesus turned our attention to the lilies of the field and the birds of the air, he acknowledged that God's providence blankets life's uncertainties and that we should concentrate on living today instead of being anxious for tomorrow. At length, lilies wither and birds die, and so will we. Death, which is simultaneously an ending and a beginning, is not worth the worry.

In retrospect, the Romantic flirtation with death in the nineteenth century appears melancholy and decadent. By aspiring to die with a "bright burning flame," poets meant to celebrate life, but often their embrace of death was only an excuse for burning their candles at both ends. Romanticism itself died in the trenches of the First World War, where death was ugly, common, and pointless. In our time, the Romantic obsession persists only among NASCAR drivers, skydivers, and adventurers addicted to sharpening life's edge.

While their intention is to be compassionate, there is nothing romantic about the Hemlock Society and Dr. Jack Kevorkian, who aim to make euthanasia an option for the terminally ill and suffering. In recent years, as mankind has gained a certain leverage over life and death, it became inevitable that this advantage would be used not only to extend life but to prevent it and end it. If birth control could be employed successfully to prevent conception, then someone was bound to embrace abortion to effectively deny life to the fetus. Extending the same principle (an individual's dominion over his or her body), a growing number of people argue for the freedom to terminate one's own life. Yet there is even more resistance to euthanasia than to abortion, and it is not difficult to fathom why. People sense uneasily that these powers over life are not creative but destructive: not life-giving but life-ending. And euthanasia is final.

Oddly enough, whereas contraception, abortion, and mercy killing are hailed as compassionate and responsible, their champions typically decry capital punishment on the principle that, while one should be free to deprive himself (or one's fetus or grandmother) of life, we are not free to tamper with the life of a serial killer. Here in Virginia, we retain capital punishment, but we also honor living wills intended to prevent doctors and hospitals from artificially prolonging anyone's misery when death is otherwise imminent and inevitable. It is not a bad choice, and indeed, it is only optional. If one wishes to cling to life no matter what, he can simply avoid a living will altogether.

## Confronting Death

The cloud that surrounds death is really the mystery of evil and, more precisely, the problem of pain. There is perhaps no satisfactory explanation for suffering, and an explanation is not really what we seek in any case. Those who use the existence of suffering to deny God's existence seek only to *avoid* pain. When that proves impossible, they blame it on the Creator.

It is people, not God, who inflict suffering on themselves and one another. Pain is also the side effect of tragic, unintended accidents. Unthinking nature, running its course like a steamroller, often leaves victims in its wake. Death is occasionally tragic, but seldom a catastrophe; most often, one's passing is a domestic and private drama. Nevertheless, over the centuries, death as a subject has attracted poets and philosophers as much as love. Thomas Mann claimed that "without death, there would scarcely have been poets on earth." Michelangelo confessed that "no thought exists in me which death has not carved with his chisel." Socrates, Plato, and Montaigne believed that the function of philosophy was to grapple with the problem of death. Elisabeth Kübler-Ross suggests that the reason our culture copes poorly with death is that we have enhanced its mystery by putting it out of our sight.

To confront death is to celebrate life; to deny death is to sleep through life. Increasingly, death is the last thing we plan for. In northern Virginia, where my family lives, historic cemeteries are preserved for our Revolutionary and Civil War dead, but scant provision is made to establish graveyards for its current inhabitants. The land, close to the nation's capital, is too valuable as a potential home site for the living to be set aside for the dead. In Washington, where I worked for many years, the prevailing preference for memorial services over funerals perpetuates the myth that one can be transformed from a living, breathing human being into a memory without the intervening inconvenience of dying. These days, bodies are routinely whisked from hospitals and nursing homes to the mortuary. The only death we witness is the remains of a hapless squirrel in the road as we speed by in our cars.

Americans were more sensible not many decades ago. My wife tells me that certain Victorian middle-class homes in New England and the Midwest were built featuring funeral doors leading directly from the street into the parlor. Her uncle's home in Ohio had such a special portal, used only for wakes. When one's home actually possessed a door for death to enter and exit, the accessory rendered death natural and not morbid. In many homes, life and death were equally notable experiences. People were born and they died not only in the same house but sometimes in the same bed. Today children are born in hospitals, not because birth is an illness, but as a precautionary measure. So with death: it is no more an illness than birth. Yet in terminal cases, people are expected to die in hospitals despite the fact that there is no medical (no health-enhancing) reason for them to be there. And the food is terrible!

## *Mourning*

Flags all around the nation's capital often fly at half-mast to honor major and minor officials who have died. These are dignified reminders of death. In the past, there were established periods of mourning; *Gone With the Wind*'s Scarlett O'Hara was forced by convention to wear black after her unloved first husband was killed in the war.

As a theological student in Paris in the sixties, I was asked for counsel by a middle-aged Frenchman wearing a black armband, the public sign of grief, regarding the death of his mother. His dilemma was that, although the traditional mourning period was not over, his wife and children were complaining that they wanted their lives to return to normal. It was the Christmas season. The kids wanted to see their friends and go to the movies; his wife wanted to wear bright clothes again and go to parties. How, he asked, could he discharge his responsibilities to both the living and the dead?

I confessed to him that I thought his predicament was more cultural and familial than religious, and being neither married nor French myself, I felt ill equipped to advise him. But being young (and he being persistent), I suggested a compromise: that he continue his own observance but release his family. I do not know what marital mischief I may have caused by that counsel, but I was impressed by the sincerity of his determination to honor his mother's memory.

The tradition of a formal period of mourning acknowledged that grief was a public matter. Survivors recognized that their personal pain and loss was acknowledged and respected by friends and strangers alike. Something similar might help persons who are terminally ill, because silence and a stiff upper lip make sorrow a private matter. But the lamentable fact is that nowadays, just as we shelter death from the living, we hide illness from the dying. Doctors and nurses informed neither my mother nor my father that they had no chance of recovery in their final months. They had to figure out the bad news themselves, then *keep* it to themselves. Sadly, my parents' experience is not uncommon in our look-away society.

While death is a release leading to transformation, dying itself can be an agony, not restricted to physical pain alone. Kübler-Ross traces five stages of dying for those with terminal illness:

Denial ("No, not me!")
Rage ("Why me?")
Bargaining ("Here's what I'll give for more time.")
Depression ("Yes, me.")
Acceptance ("My time is close and it's all right.")

She characterizes this final acceptance as something less than joy but something more than stoic resignation—a step in the right direction to accepting death as a natural process.

## "My Sister Death"

Those who recognize death as the portal to eternity will make it welcome, as Saint Francis of Assisi did when he exclaimed: "Welcome, my sister Death." Or as Garvin, a twelve-year-old English boy who died of bone marrow disease a few years ago, consoled his family, telling them that "dying is not really dying; it is just like opening an old door into a new room which is heaven."

It is easy to snicker at such speeches as so much brave dialogue contrived for Hollywood death scenes. In fact, it is only a recent development that survivors are expected to console the dying. The traditional expectation was just the other way around! Thomas More not only forgave his executioner but went to great lengths to support the spirits of his family as he approached his end. To his daughter he wrote, "Never trouble thy mind for anything that ever shall keep me in this world," reminding her that "nothing can come but that which God wills."

Judaism calls for loved ones to be present with their dying family member to express solidarity. A personal confession on the deathbed is encouraged to strengthen the faith of all, affirming that one life cycle is ending with another about to begin. The dying Jew is expected to console the living as well as being consoled in his passage.

Years ago, when my wife worked with isolated Eskimo tribes in Alaska to improve the education of their children, she came to respect and admire their culture, which extends like an umbrella over birth, life, and death. It is not uncommon for a dying native to call together the community to pray together, to construct a coffin and dig a grave, clean the house, and prepare a feast from the dying person's own stores. Like the Jew, the dying Eskimo negotiates his passage by affirming life for those he loves and must leave behind. Far from being a private secret to be hidden from a healthy world, death is celebrated as a public leave-taking that strengthens victim and survivors alike.

Such a death is witnessed not as the snuffing of a candle but as the culmination of a life of light. If, unlike heroes, we do not die with a bang, neither do we depart life with but a whimper. The Jewish Mishna notes that each of us is born crying into this world. From the infant's point of view, birth is the traumatic loss of all the security it has known in the womb. Birth is experienced by the infant as death, whereas in fact it is only the newborn's passageway to life.

## The Art of Dying

As our population ages, an extensive literature has appeared concentrating on living well in one's later years, but literature aimed at helping people to die with grace has virtually disappeared. The *Ars moriendi* (*The Art of Dying*) in fact enjoys a long literary history extending back to the ancient Egyptian and the Tibetan Book of the Dead—detailed guidebooks to the individual's passage to the afterlife. They are echoed in the Mayan Book of the Dead in pre-Columbian America.

Among Christians, the art of dying became the subject of an extensive body of popular literature beginning in the late Middle Ages, stimulated by the frequent plagues, famines, wars, and executions that rendered life uncertain and anxious. The almost palpable presence of death paralleled the decline of the church as a political and spiritual protector of the faithful. Consequently, people were thrown on their own resources to make sense of the hope given by their Savior, who long since had conquered death and promised Paradise.

The *Ars moriendi* actually taught the art of *living* in the light of certain death and cautioned against the futility of mere materialism, for, it argued, one can't bring material things to eternity. But, it added, many things can be cultivated in this life that will be possessed fully in the next, among them love, knowledge, appreciation, and even adventure. But wealth, honors, power, and lust were deemed *vanitas vanitatum* (vanity of vanities), and the faithful were urged instead to contemplate death correctively—by focusing one's life on transcendent riches encompassed in the love of God. *The Art of Dying* aimed to assist the Christian to view the present life positively in the light of eternity.

The ancient Christian practice of anointing the sick is an invitation to physical recovery, reminiscent of Jesus' cures. Over time, however, the practice degenerated into a spiritual embalming—a pious kiss of death. When the priest appeared at one's bedside, it was a sure sign that one was at death's door, all hope of recovery lost. Since the sixties, the church has restored the sacrament to its original purpose—to rally the body, if possible, or, if necessary, to prepare the spirit for the passage from life to life.

While skeptics may be inclined to cling futilely to the present life for fear of the beyond, believers can make the opposite mistake of assessing their present lives as trivial compared to eternity. In fact, both assessments are faulty. Life is but the opening act to a worthy play, and death but a brief intermission. A good act establishes the plot, the pace, and the characters for the rest of the play—and so with eternity.

## Hidden Lives and Unvisited Tombs

After we die, the lives of most of us will be celebrated for but a generation by those who shared our table, our friendship, or our bed. But in the eternal scheme of things, we will be more than a memory: we will have made a mark for good or ill. And perhaps even the world will be better off for our brief sojourn here. George Eliot might have had us in mind when she wrote in *Middlemarch*: "[The] growing good of the world is partly dependent on unhistoric acts; and that things are not so ill with you and me as they might have been is half owing to the number who lived faithfully a hidden life, and rest in unvisited tombs."

Those who live the present life in the light of eternity do not fear the Grim Reaper. Rather, like convivial pub dwellers who have had their fill, they are prepared to roll home when the proprietor announces, "Time, gentlemen, please!" If that simile strikes you as too secular and English, then exchange it for the graceful exit of old Simeon in the gospel, who, having held the infant Jesus in his arms, exclaimed: "At last, Lord, you can dismiss your servant in peace, as you promised. For with my eyes I have seen your salvation" (Luke 2:29–30).

Our life's greatest adventure is still ahead of us.

# ENTER LAUGHING

Toto, I don't think we're in Kansas anymore.

DOROTHY, IN

*THE WIZARD OF OZ*

In Tibet, the bar-headed goose and gander perform an unusual ceremony after mating. They rise together from the waters, wings outthrust and flapping, beaks turned straight to the sky, honking loudly. These geese have a life span of half a century and celebrate their perpetuation of life in the same way every year. When one dies, its partner never mates again.

The peninsula across the lake from our home is too shallow for suburban developers, but friendly to Canadian geese, who find it so accommodating that they have ceased their seasonal migration and have become, in effect, U.S. citizens. They mate and raise their goslings, sojourning as families on the water. At sunrise and sunset they take to the air in precise formations, honking in high spirits, flying for no particular reason and toward no particular destination, but simply for the joy of being alive.

It is risky to assign a sense of humor to animals. But some species—like the geese—surely know joy, perhaps because they (better than we) mine the present moment of its blessings. The only way to treat life with the seriousness it deserves is with a sense of humor. Unlike humans, animals live unburdened by regret for the past and anxiety about the future. Instinctively and innocently, they live in the present moment and exult in it.

If we learn to emulate them, we will enter eternity laughing.

ॐ

ON NOVEMBER 18, 1973, a thirty-one-year-old mother of seven children was readied for a routine partial hysterectomy. By the time she left the hospital, she had experienced an adventure that was anything but routine.

Betty Eadie's heritage was half Native American. A sign in front of the Brainerd Indian Training School, where she studied, proclaimed, "Where there is no vision, the people perish." Little could Betty's Methodist missionary teachers have predicted the vision their student would experience as an adult: by her own account, she died, went to heaven, then returned to everyday life during the course of her operation.

On resuming domestic responsibilities, Betty found herself a different person, struggling to transform her life in the light of the eternity she had briefly visited. Not long after her return from the hospital, she painted the living room of her home bright orange, prompting her consternated husband to remark that neighbors thought the house was on fire.

Having tasted joy beyond description, Betty plummeted back to earth and everyday life. She felt exiled from Paradise—depressed, anxious, and humorless, chronically fatigued, forgetting about hygiene, and neglecting her appearance. Her solitary solace was prayer. Over time, she came to accept that her near-death experience was no substitute for faith, and she grew determined to become a healer.

Betty became adept at hypnotherapy and used it to ease the delivery of her daughter's first child. As she grew in strength, she found herself sensitive to others' thoughts and feelings, and developed a degree of clairvoyance. Until she could return to heaven at life's end, she vowed to live by the rules of unconditional love and forgiveness and by letting go of her concern for tomorrow. Reconciled to the fact that heaven would have to wait, she developed a sense of humor and a lighthearted seriousness. When she next makes the trip, one-way, she will enter eternity laughing.

In 1992, nearly twenty years after her incredible journey, Betty Eadie recounted the experience in two books, *Embraced by the Light* and *The Awakening Heart.* Both became publishing sensations, and unleashed a torrent of accounts by others who had survived similar near-death experiences.

## *An Incredible Journey*

Nothing in her life had prepared Betty for her experience, which was more awe inspiring than joyous. On the operating table, seemingly dead, she felt herself plunged into darkness, "as if I had been swallowed up by an enormous tornado" moving her faster than the speed of light, yet leaving her tranquil and at peace. She was not alone in racing toward a pinpoint of light, which revealed itself to be at the end of a dark tunnel. Other people, and animals as well, were swept up with her, moving parallel to her at a distance from her path.

Accelerating toward the light, she reported,

I was instinctively attracted to it, although . . . I felt that others might not be. As I approached it, I noticed the figure of a man standing in it, with the light radiating all around him. . . . Although his light was much brighter than my own, I was aware that my light, too, illuminated us. As our lights emerged, I felt as if I had stepped into his countenance, and I felt an utter explosion of love.

She sensed at once that the man was Jesus, "who had always loved me, even when I thought he hated me." Of a sudden, she realized that her life was woven from a single fabric, and that everything that happens, good and bad, contributes to a mission one is given in life: "I understood that life is lived most fully in the imagination—that, ironically, imagination is the key to reality." She did not, however, believe her experience to be a fantasy.

In conversation with Jesus, she discovered to her relief that he has a sense of humor, "delightful and quick as any here—far more so." He introduced her to aspects of the afterlife. Some inhabitants toiled at looms, weaving celestial clothing. Betty visited a garden as ethereal as a rainbow, whose waters and plants possessed intelligence and praised God. Contemplating a single living rose, she found herself literally absorbed within it, concluding that "we were all one."

## Life's Mysteries Answered

Not content merely to experience eternity, Betty asked Jesus questions and got answers. She learned that most people choose the illnesses they suffer in life, but that even unpleasant experiences are potentially good. Death is "graduation" into eternity. However, many spirits remain on earth to comfort the bereaved, and still others stay earthbound because they resist moving on. These restless spirits will keep themselves from eternity "until they learn to accept the greater power around them and to let go of the world." Prayer, she was told, is a beacon between time and eternity.

Eternity, Betty learned, satisfies each spirit in a way unique to that individual. But the adventure has a dark side. Satan seeks to deter us from the light but lacks God's power to read our thoughts. Although she was not punished for it, Betty was confronted with the ripple effect of the harm she had already caused others in life. On her eternal journey she also encountered spirits of persons not yet born. One person-to-be was in the process of trying to attract his prospective parents into marriage. Another chose to be conceived as mentally handicapped. Birth, he conceded with equanimity, "is a sleep and a forgetting."

Although she resisted her return to earth and time, Betty was informed that she had an unfinished mission, although the memory of its details and of much she experienced in eternity was to be blotted out. She concludes: "I have simply been impressed to live within the light of Jesus Christ and to continue to accept his love in my life"—and to share his humor.

### Love and Laughter

Betty Eadie's account is remarkable for its detail, her curiosity, and the impact it has made on her life and the lives of those around her. By contrast, most accounts of near-death experiences are sketchy and passive. They also lack the specific religious imagery of her adventure in the afterlife. Psychiatrist Raymond A. Moody Jr. notes that although the experience of light is "invariable" in these accounts, the identity given to the light varies widely, and the heaven that many people describe bears faint resemblance to the one they were taught about in Sunday school.

Betty's heaven is clearly Christian, but not traditionally so. She is content to simply identify Jesus as God, whereas Jesus clearly distinguished between himself, his Father, and the Holy Spirit. It is likely that a trained theologian or a saint would deliver a more nuanced report of the afterlife. But that is not to discount Betty's experience, or those of other untrained observers. We all bring preconceptions and blind spots to our lives; why not to eternity?

If I were to take an astronaut's place in a space journey, I would perforce return to earth with a stunted and naive account, but one that was true to what I saw and could crudely interpret. Heaven is clearly not a standard-issue product but is experienced uniquely by each person according to his or her education, ability, sentiments, and even sense of humor.

Australian researcher Dr. Sherie Sutherland studied a large group of near-death survivors who reported their experience of eternity. On average, her subjects were less religious than the general population *prior to* their experience, and became even less convinced of the value of organized religion *after* their taste of eternity. Whereas 38 percent of her subjects were churchgoers before their adventure, only 20 percent continued to attend church afterward. However, following their experience, virtually all practiced meditation, sought spiritual guidance, and pursued spiritual values in their lives. In her book *Reborn in the Light* Dr. Sutherland notes: "They now have an ongoing contact with Good or a Higher Power that requires no mediation by institutions such as the Church or interpretation by the teachings of any denomination or tradition."

One of her subjects characterized her experience as "Knowing God. *Really* knowing. And that's the thing that I can't, that I feel sad I can't really share with people I know. That's the big thing that changes your whole life." Another drew this lesson: "Love, love. Love is the most important feeling in the universe. . . . And sometimes the feeling is so strong it makes me cry, sometimes it makes me laugh. Whichever way you look at it, it's just fantastic!"

## The Relevance of Laughter

When Charles Darwin was asked what characteristic distinguishes humans from the beasts, the father of evolution replied that *Homo sapiens* alone blush. Human folly makes life a comedy. Without the beasts' instincts to guide us, we humans lose our bearings, paint ourselves into corners, and slip on metaphorical banana peels. Others laugh at our embarrassment; we blush.

In ancient times, when Aristotle was asked the same question, he had a related answer. The Greek philosopher identified the distinctive human trait as laughter. Only men and women among the creatures possess a sense of humor. Clearly, the scientist and the philosopher were both right, inasmuch as humor and embarrassment share the same roots. We either blush or laugh at the disparity between our goals and our achievements, our vanities and our pitfalls, our reach and our grasp. Without shame, we would be monsters, blindly indulging our basest passions. Without humor, we would find life (and ourselves) a chronic disappointment. Humor affirms that life has meaning, and embarrassment arises because we are measured against ideals not of our own making. If life were truly pointless and we were only creatures of habit, there would be no need or place for laughter or shame. For those of us who have yet to see the light, laughter will be the price of admission. The purpose of shame is to prompt us to laugh at ourselves and to clean up our act.

## Laughing at the Devil

Two aged comedians are resting in the garden of the Actors Fund Nursing and Retirement Home, forty-five minutes from Broadway. One is reed thin and pale, the other portly and pinkish; they are reminiscent of Laurel and Hardy or Abbott and Costello. "I'm a frustrated comedian," confesses the thin one loudly. "You ever hear of Bob Hope? Well, I'm his brother: No Hope." His companion groans. "Stop with that joke," he pleads.

There are about one hundred aged actors and actresses at the actors' retirement home. Anyone who can prove that he or she performed in vaudeville or even worked behind the scenes in a Broadway theater is eligible for entry. Few of the residents are able to pay the $80-a-day fee for room and board, so the fund picks up the tab for most of them. Although few of the actors were comics on the stage, humor nevertheless rules the day. "Let's face it, this is not a happy solution for anybody," confides an eighty-nine-year-old former Denishawn dancer. "But every day you can get up and you have all your marbles and are able to walk and you have something to do—well, it's just fine."

Another former dancer approaching ninety agrees: "The more you read about galaxies sixty billion light-years away, the more you think, What the hell do we matter? Except that you have to matter, because you have to live." She delivers this wisdom with laughter.

In a New York SoHo loft, twenty-five people not connected with show business are also laughing. Unlike the Broadway veterans at the actors' retirement home, many of these are young, but most will beat the oldsters to eternity. All have AIDS, cancer, or another terminal illness, and many are in pain.

They are laughing at newspaper accounts read to them by a fifty-four-year-old woman, Ganga Stone. She reads a clipping about a woman swept to her death by a gigantic wave just as she was scattering her mother's ashes in the Pacific. "And here's one of my favorites," Stone chuckles as she quotes a clipping about two evangelists mashed in a parking lot by a crashing plane. "Get this—the husband was in the *extermination business!*"

Her class erupts in laughter at Stone's black humor, many of them in spite of themselves. They want to feel sorry for themselves in their solitary plight, but she won't let them wallow in tragedy, insisting that they make their final journey laughing.

One young man, Victor, knows he will die of AIDS as his lover did, and he's uncertain about an afterlife. He resents Stone's hope and humor, because it robs him of his grief and makes his coming death appear trivial, when he wants it to be high drama. But Victor keeps returning to her classes in life affirmation, which are the centerpiece of an organization called God's Love We Deliver, which boasts a $5.3 million budget, sixty-three full-time staffers, and more than two-thousand volunteers, who deliver over a thousand meals and smiles a day to the terminally ill.

Laurie Goodstein of *The Washington Post* notes that Stone not only helps her students to exit this life laughing but also prepares them to help their sick friends make the crossing to eternity in good humor. One class member, Kip Reynolds, forty-three and HIV-positive himself, kept vigil at the bedside of a friend dying of AIDS. Comfortingly, he whispered, "Relax, go to the light . . . You're going to get rid of this painful body." Goodstein reports that when his friend's breathing slowed, then stopped, Victor knew his friend was gone: "Not dead, just gone somewhere else. Hopefully, he thought to himself, to Hawaii. And he laughed."

## The Absence of Laughter

Life, of course, is not a joke. Still, humor puts life's vagaries in perspective and is our closest companion to hope. If we exit laughing, we will enter eternity with a smile.

For many people, smiles do not come easily. Not long before her own death, Mother Teresa recounted her visit to a comfortable nursing home in America and contrasted it with the experience of the destitute in her own Calcutta clinic:

> I can never forget the experience I had in the sitting room where they kept all these old parents of sons and daughters who had just put them into an institution and forgotten

them, maybe. In that home, these old people had everything—good food, comfortable place, television, everything—but everyone was looking toward the door. And I did
not see a single smile on their face. I turned to a sister and I
asked, "Why do these people who have every comfort . . . why
are they not smiling? I'm so used to seeing the smiles on our
people. Even the dying ones smile." And Sister said, "This is
the way it is nearly every day. They are expecting, they are
hoping that the son or the daughter will come to visit them.
They are hurt because they are forgotten."

Laughter feeds on love, and the lowliest who pass into eternity
from Mother Teresa's clinic know that they are loved.

## Nervous Laughter

In the course of penning these pages, I have rediscovered what I
already knew: that life is precious and real, and that death is inevitable. Humanity, composed of flesh and blood, possesses a
spirit that, having tasted life, is not content with oblivion. If it is
vanity to expect that life, once given, will never end, then it is
God's vanity, not ours, because we are *his* idea, conceived and con-
served by him. I have also shared a fresh discovery with you: that
those who have tasted death already lose their fear of it, embrace
life, and look confidently to its fulfillment in eternity. They smile
and laugh in hope, whereas the rest of us manage only nervous
laughter in the face of the unknown.

But we are not in the dark. Common sense suggests that the
Creator, having crafted us for his own purposes, will not cast us
aside like a child abandoning his toys. Instead, he will sustain us.
Faith has greater expectations, proposing (against the evidence of
our occasional perversity and routine indifference) that it is in
God's own interest to preserve us, because his sole motivation for

creation is love. The Creator alone knows the pattern from which we were made, and he accepts the flaws we have introduced into his design. As products of his manufacture, we may be irregulars or seconds, but we are not rejects, because our Designer accepts us.

Christianity asserts an even more radical cause for joy and motivation for laughter. It holds that each man, woman, and child who has ever been, or ever will be, is created in God's image. For God to abandon the least of us would be to abandon himself. This is borne out in the parable of the Good Shepherd: no sheep will be lost. The more we think of ourselves as dim sheep, forever wandering off, the more we will grasp the humor of life's journey and welcome the Shepherd's guidance.

Eternity may begin while we are still babes in arms. My twin daughters, born two months premature with only a slim hold on life, were baptized by the hospital chaplain within minutes of entering the world. They are now healthy adult women. Their elder sister suffered grand mal seizures as an infant and was judged by doctors to have no hold on life. She, too, is now a healthy and productive adult. Although death lurked at the outset of these three lives so close to my own, heaven is still ahead of them. All three daughters navigate lives with disabilities, but their spirits have not flagged and their sense of humor is not impaired.

## Liturgy and Laughter

My daughters were baptized into hope and joy. That Christian initiation mimics death and resurrection. It is a ritual death that leads to life. When John the Baptist immersed converts in the waters of the River Jordan, it was intended to suggest death by drowning—no laughing matter. But what dies symbolically in baptism is the self-will and perversity inherited from Adam and Eve. What emerges from the waters is a new being, a new creation, no longer a stranger expelled from Paradise but a child of

God destined for heaven. The message is clear in the prayers pronounced during infant baptisms: "Grant that the old Adam in this
child may be so buried that the new man may be raised up in
him." That is cause for joy.

Where theology and imagination falter, ritual succeeds in expressing the Christian optimism. One of the most memorable experiences of my life was conducting the graveside services for my
wife's parents, who died within months of each other. I used the
rite specified in the Book of Common Prayer, which begins:
"Happy from now on are those who die in the Lord!" The deceased
has gone to a heaven "where sorrow and pain are no more, neither
sighing, but life everlasting." At great funerals a choir takes up
the anthem "Into paradise may the angels lead you."

The ritual is ancient, reflecting eras when life was more of a trial
than it is today with modern medicine, conveniences, and forty-
hour workweeks. In ages past, death was viewed not only as the portal to eternal happiness but as an escape from the burdens of daily
toil. Hence the emphasis on eternal rest rather than joy. If there is no
laughter at funerals, it is because the sorrow of the bereaved pre-
dominates over the joy of one more person joining the majority.

Of course, there are people who look upon life as nothing more
than a cosmic joke; they choke on their laughter, despairing. For
the faithful, however, laughter is the natural companion of hope,
optimism, gratitude, and joy. Long ago, G. K. Chesterton affirmed that "joy is the gigantic secret of the Christian" and speculated that Jesus hid something when he went up a mountain to
pray. "I have sometimes fancied that it was his mirth," he said.

## Laughing at Ourselves

Ole Anthony, founder of the Dallas-based Trinity Foundation and
publisher of "the world's pretty much only religious satire maga-

zine" (the *Door*), agrees with Chesterton. "If it were not for the medicine of created laughter," he argues, "there would be no antidote to pride and vanity among men. . . . The problem is that most religious people seem to have been out to lunch when funnybones were being distributed. Instead, you find them pushing around a karmic wheelbarrow of rigidity, hypocrisy, pomposity, presumption and pretense."

Anthony's community of lay men and women not only feed and house the homeless in Dallas but get them to laugh at the human predicament. When people can laugh at themselves, he notes, they have found the key to redemption. The mission of his magazine is "to make people think through laughter, to carve up sacred cows, to humble the haughty, and to challenge all people to fully test and question what they hold sacred." Those who cultivate the habit of laughter now will be armed with it when they enter eternity, where laughter is a way of life.

Of course, laughter is not the only key to open eternity. In our present lives, we catch brief glimpses of eternity when art or love or nature frees us from the prison of our egos for precious instants, rewarding us with unexpected moments of transcendence. Kindness is another key. When we show compassion we are most like God; in those moments we can best understand him because we are acting as he does: out of love. Then we begin to discern the Creator in the creatures he made in his image. And we can begin to laugh together.

I recently came across the eulogy delivered by playwright Alan Bennett at the 1995 memorial service for his friend the satirist Peter Cook. Cook was a man of massive appetites who, unrepentant, drank, ate, medicated, and womanized himself to death at the age of fifty-eight. "In the press coverage of [Cook's] death," Bennett noted, "one could detect a certain satisfaction—the feeling that he had paid some sort of price for his gifts, had died in the way the press prefer funny men to die . . . sad and disappointed."

In fact, Cook died laughing, not least at himself. Bennett called him "a figure from the parables, a publican, a sinner, but never a Pharisee—the message of a character like Peter's being that a life of complete self-indulgence, if led with the whole heart, may also bring wisdom."

Laughter, far from being scornful, is an expression of respect for life. Laughter celebrates life and affirms hope. When comedian Benny Hill died, the church of Saint Martin-in-the-Fields overflowed with people who had known the comic only through his television programs, at the end of which he was invariably pursued by a mob of police, cuckolded husbands, and women outraged by his lusty misdemeanors. When they appeared on television, these chases were speeded up in the manner of Keystone Kops films. In a fitting tribute to Hill, the throngs leaving his memorial service chased one another around Trafalgar Square, all the while laughing.

## Finding Faith, Keeping Faith

Theology, properly defined, is faith seeking understanding—*not* faith demanding certainty. An informed faith equips the believer to be in life's driver's seat, knowing his destination; still, doubt is always a passenger. It is my experience, however, that faith is more vulnerable to indifference than to doubt. It is one thing to worry over one's beliefs, quite another to throw in the towel and stop caring. The sensible seeker prays with the apostle Thomas: "I believe; help my unbelief."

Jesus' own resurrection has always been the essential ingredient of the Christian faith—the engine of faith. But the expectation of life after death is not the property of Christianity alone. It is shared by adherents of other religious faiths and by those men and women who, dismissive of organized religion, have nevertheless experienced moments of transcendence in this life through art, music, literature, nature, and love. God, after all, is not a Christian, nor is he the prisoner of any religion. He is above all faiths and all doubts, having planted a love of life and a yearning for eternity in us all—including those who doubt his existence.

Faithful or skeptical, most of us would prefer to place our bets on an afterlife rather than on oblivion. But what if the prospect is only a pipe dream? What if, once asleep, we never awaken?

## Betting on Eternity

More than three centuries ago, the philosopher Blaise Pascal (1623–62) attempted to answer these questions with a wager that goes like this: If you believe in God and there is indeed a God, you win eternal happiness. On the other hand, if you believe in God and he turns out to be a myth, you lose nothing. But if you reject faith in God, and he does exist, then you lose for all eternity. Pascal's conclusion: the only losers are those who reject God.

Gambling on God has never attracted me. It assumes that the object of faith is to cash in on an eternal payoff. Moreover, Pascal's wager suggests that God punishes people who, for whatever reason, lack faith. That will not do either. But give the philosopher his due. He was writing at a time when Christian living involved great sacrifices and when those who turned from religion did so to pursue lives of sensuality and corruption. With his wager, Pascal was simply reassuring people who believed in God that it was a good bet to follow God's will. He didn't address the good person who, for whatever reason, didn't share his faith.

Let's take the worst-case scenario. Suppose that when our lives end, that's all there is. First off, we won't realize the loss because there will no longer be a "we" to experience it. Alone, that wouldn't justify our having lived lives of self-deception, but look at it this way: integrity and love are their own rewards. It is sane to be faithful, sensible to be compassionate, and gratifying to be grateful. Everyone who truly relishes life will revere it and be responsible to it, whatever his or her faith.

I hope not to lose Pascal's wager, but my faith is not just a bet on an afterlife. Rather, I am betting on a God who sent his Son to live this life with us, to die for us, and to transform himself and us in the process. That is no pipe dream.

If you do not share my religious faith, we still share the same Creator, the same aspirations, and the same destiny. There is no onus to being a reluctant believer or searching skeptic. I share your diffidence. It is sensible to be skeptical, and to shrink from something as complicated as faith, and from someone as demanding as God. Nevertheless, there is wisdom in the saying that unless we stand for something, we will fall for anything. I applaud you for wishing to be better informed about our common destiny, and I trust that any remaining ambivalence stems more from your natural fear of the unknown and less from your uncertainty about details of your faith.

The epistle to the Hebrews states that "faith means putting our full confidence in the things we hope for; it means being certain of things we cannot see" (11:1). In other words, faith gives substance to our hope and vision to our love. And love is eternal.

The fear of every person who struggles with faith, hope, and doubt is well founded, and I share it with you. But to know God is to love him, and love conquers timidity. Grace abounds and, if we let it, will transform us into new creatures suited for eternity. The proper attitude toward life is gratitude and humor. Begin extracting the most from each moment. Live each moment in the light of eternity.

Should fate decree that you and I never meet in the course of this life, I fondly look forward to catching up with you in the next. Unless I miss my guess, we will both be laughing.

# EPILOGUE

So, WHAT CAN WE CONCLUDE ABOUT ETERNITY? SURELY IT IS in some sense a place, not just a state of being, because we will enter the afterlife whole (as Jesus did), not as disembodied spirits. Whereas God is complete as a spirit, we are not.

But to conceive of heaven as a reconstituted Paradise presents problems. Eden was created for physical creatures, whereas heaven is home to God and the angels as well, and they are spirits. Clearly, heaven must be made to suit us all.

Probably the best definition of heaven is the oldest: closeness with our Creator. It was the rejection of that intimacy that necessitated Jesus' death and resurrection. Whatever its landscape and furnishings, heaven is not ours by right but by gift. Like our very lives, it is unearned. Hell is a rejection of God's generosity—the persistence of Adam's choice of self over God. Hell is for the uncommitted and the ungrateful. Love has no place in hell.

Although purgatory has no basis in revelation, I incline with C. S. Lewis to the notion that few of us depart this life wholly prepared for what God has in store for us. Just as life is full of second chances to accept or reject redemption, it follows that there might be a kind of apprenticeship for us after death to regain our bearings and our integrity, readying us for an eternity with God. If such a purgatory exists, we are not condemned to it, but will choose it freely because we want to enter heaven wholeheartedly, dressed for the occasion, ready to mix with that society.

I am neither prophet nor seer, but only a guide to what others (saints among them) have speculated about our common destiny. Still, some intimations of our immortality are better expressed than others. When my wife's father died, we could find no better tribute to him than verses taken from *Adonais,* Shelley's elegy on the death of John Keats. It is my favorite rendering of eternity:

> He lives, he wakes—'tis Death is dead, not he . . .
> . . . . . . . . . . . . . . . . . . . . . .
> He is made one with Nature: there is heard
> His voice in all her music, from the moan
> Of thunder, to the song of night's sweet bird . . .
> . . . . . . . . . . . . . . . . . .
> He is a portion of the loveliness
> Which once he made more lovely . . .
> . . . . . . . . . . . . . . . . .
> That Light whose smile kindles the Universe,
> That Beauty in which all things work and move,
> That Benediction which the eclipsing Curse
> Of birth can quench not, that sustaining Love
> Which through the web of being blindly wove
> By man and beast and earth and air and sea,
> Burns bright or dim, as each are mirrors of
> The fire for which all thirst; now beams on me . . .
> . . . . . . . . . . . . . . . . . . . . . .
> my spirit's bark is driven,
> Far from the shore, far from the trembling throng
> Whose sails were never to the tempest given;

The massy earth and spherèd skies are riven!
I am borne darkly, fearfully, afar;
Whilst, burning through the inmost veil of Heaven,
The soul of Adonais, like a star,
Beacons from the abode where the Eternal are.

# ACKNOWLEDGMENTS

IN HELPING TO SHATTER THE SILENCE OF SERIOUS CONTEMPO-rary literature concerning the afterlife, I have depended on many other authors, who are acknowledged as they appear in these pages. Nearly all of them have long since joined the majority who entered eternity before us. However, two books by living authors proved to be indispensable and deserve to be singled out: the encyclopedic *Heaven: A History* by Colleen McDannell and Bernhard Lang (Yale University Press, 1988) and the charming *I Will See You in Heaven,* edited by Michael Seed (St. Paul Publications, 1991). Other selected sources appear as recommended reading at the end of the book. There is nothing to compare with reading the originals.

If books are part of our eternal reward, I expect that my dependable editors Fred Hills and Hilary Black and copy editor Chuck Antony will be inspiring the heavenly host, correcting their grammar and checking their facts as they did mine. Over many rewrites, they have made the text more accessible and, I trust, more useful for readers who are unwilling to simply wait for eternity but wish to live the present moment in its light. Thanks, too, to Fred's assistant, Priscilla Holmes, to my lawyer-agent, Ron Goldfarb. I can't think of a better advocate before the bar of heaven.

My wife, Rebecca, is quoted only occasionally in these pages but is nevertheless my most important source and resource. Becky's grasp of history, literature, biography, and the arts gave human dimension to what otherwise might have been a dry essay in religion. I am blessed to share my life with a person I constantly learn from. It is my fondest hope to spend eternity with her.

DAVID YOUNT
Montclair, Virginia
August 1998

# FURTHER READING

A S A CASUAL READER MYSELF, I AM SLIGHTLY RESENTFUL OF the bibliographies that burden scholarly books. I already feel pretty proud of myself for having gotten through whatever book I have just handled and do not need to be told to read others. Moreover, whenever I announce that I have started writing on a subject, I am besieged by persons who insist: "You can't possibly write a book about X until you have read Y and Z." Such well-intentioned advice is guaranteed to produce writer's block and a serious case of insecurity.

Nevertheless, I could not have written the pages you have just read without the wisdom I found elsewhere, so I share a few highly recommended sources with you.

Saint Augustine. *The City of God.* Doubleday Image, 1958.

*The Book of Common Prayer.* Seabury Press, 1979.

Stanislav Grof. *Books of the Dead: Manuals for Living and Dying.* Thames & Hudson, 1994.

Hans Küng. *Eternal Life?* SCM Press, 1984.

C. S. Lewis. *The Great Divorce.* Macmillan, 1946.

Colleen McDannell and Bernhard Lang. *Heaven: A History.* Yale University Press, 1988.

Michael Seed, ed. *I Will See You in Heaven.* St. Paul Publications, 1991.

Alice K. Turner. *The History of Hell.* Harcourt Brace & Co., 1993.

# READER REQUEST

I am gathering material for a forthcoming book that explores the experience of *redemption* in people's lives. If you have had your life transformed by grace—or know someone who has—I invite you to share your story with me. It can help others find hope. I promise to acknowledge your contribution. Please let me know whether I may use your name.

Contact me at P.O. Box 2758, Woodbridge, VA 22193, or at *dyount@erols.com*. Visit me at my Web site: *www.erols.com/dyount*.